THE PROGRESSIVE PLANTER

THE PROGRESSIVE PLANTER

A Handbook for Ecclesial Entrepreneurs

Joe Graves

Abingdon Press
Nashville

THE PROGRESSIVE PLANTER:
A HANDBOOK FOR ECCLESIAL ENTREPRENEURS

ISBN: 9781791040116
Library of Congress Control Number: 2025937173

MANUFACTURED IN THE UNITED STATES OF AMERICA

Contents

Foreword

One would think that after spending 27 ½ years as a pastor, I would know my way around a church, but after leaving the church I co-planted in the summer 2024 and beginning work as a denominational staff member supporting local churches, I came to a quick realization: I often don't know where I'm going. Literally.

I've walked up to more than one church these last few months with the intention of attending worship, but I often feel like I'm a contestant in the old "Let's Make a Deal" game show where the host would say there were prizes behind doors 1, 2, and 3. I would approach the church and realize, there are so many doors. I'd try one door. Locked. I'd try a second door. Also locked. Thankfully (so far), I've eventually made it into every church, but even when I enter, I wonder, now where do I go? All these experiences have given me new appreciation for people who are visiting church for the first time. It's also made me grateful when a church is intentional about making entry as easy as possible. One church I visited had a clear sign that said, "Are you visiting today? Start here." My slight anxiety was alleviated when I felt seen and understood. Yes, I'm new. No, I don't know where to go. But someone has acknowledged that feeling and given me a much-needed guide.

Planting a new church is a daunting process to say the least. I started planting what would become a multi-site United Methodist Church in 2009 along with a planting partner and friend and I still often felt like I didn't know where I was going and what I was doing. I was grateful for a "church planting boot camp" that sensed those fears and did all it could to spell things out in simple, step-by-step processes: Here's how you let people know about this new church you're starting. Here's how to raise money. Here's how to find spaces to meet. Of course, church planting is a linear endeavor, but I was relieved for this opportunity to learn and for someone to say, "Start here."

This is why I'm grateful for this book that you're reading. Joe Graves also knows those fears and doubts among burgeoning church planters and has created a vital resource to help people along the way. He spells things out in intuitively helpful ways so that you won't get overwhelmed and can take things in small steps, all the while building healthy systems. Joe writes, "You're not just a trailblazer, you're a trail builder."

Before he jumps into the "how-to's," though, Joe lays some important groundwork. As I was reading about motivations for church planting, I thought, "How did Joe read my mind?" I confess that a small (well, maybe not so small) motivation that we had early on was a one-sided feud with another church. There was a non-denominational church in Chicago starting at the same time as ours. They had an amazing website and seemingly cool people who were a part of it. I was envious and can neither confirm nor deny our occasional but unhealthy desire to CRUSH THEM. I counsel readers to take these early chapters seriously. Don't just jump ahead. Getting a handle and praying about the "why" you're doing this will give you a solid foundation. By doing this, you can begin to trust that God will bring people to you. Joe writes, "Can I share with you some of the best news a church planter can hear? It's simple, but if you take adequate time to ponder it and let it sink into your soul, you will find great comfort in these words: If God is calling you, God is also calling people to join you."

I'm also grateful that Joe doesn't shy away from the importance of raising funds. It's not just about funding your church. He reminds us that how we think about being generous with our finances is actually a spiritual practice and discipline. When we were starting out as planters, I was impressed with how other non-denominational planters were thinking and talking about money and thought, "Why don't United Methodists talk about this more often?" Joe has done that here.

In the end, though, you feel like you have a real ally and friend both cheering you on and praying for you. Joe shares his vulnerability and struggles while also highlighting the amazing things that planting can bring about. He's been through all of it and the lessons he has learned and is sharing are invaluable.

I couldn't have said it better than when Joe wrote, "A church planter has to wish things into existence in a world that prefers for things to remain as they are. Anyone who does anything new will face people who tell you 'That's not how it's done.' Do it anyway." Amen. You can start by turning the page and diving in. The doors will open as you do so.

Rev. Christian Coon, Northern Illinois Conference Director of Congregational Development & Co-Founder of Urban Village Church

Preface

A couple of things to know about me.

First, I'm autistic. I like starting out this way because it helps people make sense of who I am and the way I think.

Sometimes people talk about *thinking outside the box*. To be autistic is to be oblivious there is a box. While many people work hard to think *outside of the box*, we spend most of our life trying to figure out where the box is. I might say things that feel wildly normal to myself, but deeply challenging to you, and because they seem normal to me, I can be painfully casual about them. In other words, I can be blunt. I don't mean anything by this; my brain just works differently. I've learned to give myself grace, and I hope you can too—not just for me but to all of the autistic leaders out there who are leading and writing and changing the world for the better.

The other thing about autism is that we have special interests, and we can bore you with all the fine details of our special interest. If you want to learn something, find an autistic person who specializes in it, and they can tell you everything you want to know about that subject! Starting new things is one of my special interests. I *love* starting things, but of them all, none has been more challenging—or more rewarding—than starting a church. To build a fully-functioning community of people from scratch while keeping our theology intact required more than starting any other type of program or organization—more even than starting a new family.

I love everything about every part of it. So much so, that I want nothing more than to share it with you. I wish we could sit down every week and talk together about all these ideas. That's what this handbook is about. It's everything I wish I had time to explain to you one-on-one; and everything I wish I had known when I started.

I'm also a millennial which means I'm part of the "bridge generation." I was born in a world without internet or cell-service and learned to adapt to these advancements as I grew up. In the religious landscape, millennials are bridges in other ways. Many have grown up in evangelical spaces only to leave, forced to rebuild their faith. That was my experience, as a person of faith, pastor, and church planter. My church planting journey began by reading and learning from evangelicals. It was in the process of planting; with the rise of the Christian right, the killing of George Floyd, and my experience of making new LGBTQ+ friends, I began to deconstruct my allegiance to evangelicalism. We launched the year Trump was first elected, forcing us, and many others on the fringes of evangelicalism, to give it up entirely.

Through the first few years of church planting, my wife and I, along with our church community (at least the ones who stayed), had to learn how to rebuild our faith. We now find ourselves on the other side of evangelicalism, embracing the traditions of the United Methodist Church, the full inclusion of all people, the commitment to anti-racism, and the belief that Jesus is still the best way to change the world—and ourselves. This book hopes to bridge the evangelical strategies in church planting with the progressive theology we now call home. While I have much to critique about the evangelical church, there is also much we can learn from them. They are far more strategic, intentional, generous, and committed to the work of church planting, and because of this, they have figured out lots of tips and tricks that can help us plant more progressive churches that make the world a better place.

Acknowledgments

Planting a church is never a solo endeavor, and this book—like the church it describes—would not exist without the support, wisdom, and partnership of so many people.

Paul Risler and Central Avenue UMC, your support made all the difference—this wouldn't have happened without you. Because of your leadership, mentoring, and encouragement, I've grown into a pretty good pastor.

Bishop Palmer, thank you for taking a risk on us and believing in what we could build. Tim Bias, Linda Middelberg, and Dennis Miller, your leadership, advocacy, and guidance as district superintendents played a crucial role in making this church a reality.

Brad Aycock, you took a chance on us as your first church plant in West Ohio, walking with us every step of the way—even serving as the emergency contact for our son Finn at one point (which says it all). Sue Nilson Kibbey, your encouragement and support left a lasting impact during my time in seminary and through your leadership in the conference.

Roz Picardo, your eBook on the story of Embrace UMC, was one of the first and few UMC church planting books available to me. Your honesty, and willingness to share your struggles and failures, have inspired me to do the same in this book.

Rev. Steve Fewell, your generosity in opening the doors of St. Luke's for our church to share space provided critical support during one of our most difficult seasons.

Rev. Christian Coon, your coaching through a particularly challenging time and ongoing support as I sought publication for this book made a world of difference.

Max Saniel-Barney, you were the first person to say "yes" to joining our launch team. Your early encouragement and partnership meant everything.

And finally, to Allyssa Graves, my wife and co-planter: We've weathered the hardest seasons of our life together, often while planting a church (and then two more churches after that, not to mention numerous nonprofits), but we survived—and I can't wait to see what we will build together next.

To everyone who has walked alongside us—thank you. This church, this book, and this journey wouldn't have been the same without you.

Introduction

As the popular proverb states, "The best time to plant a tree was 20 years ago. The second-best time is now." The same is true for church planting.

Church attendance has seen a dramatic decline in America, with an increasing number of churches closing their doors each year. With empty church buildings and new generations looking for a place to explore their faith, there has never been a better time to start new churches.

While there are plenty of evangelical resources for this process, there are very few that are presented from a broader, more inclusive theological lens. *The Progressive Planter* walks denominational leaders, pastors, and church planters through an intentional process on how to start (or re-start) churches that are life-giving, inclusive, and rooted in emotionally healthy theology.

This handbook draws on personal experience in church planting to offer a blend of practical advice and thoughtful theological reflection, and stories from a variety of church planters. To protect privacy, some names, dates, and identifying details have been modified. Many of the stories are based on the experiences my wife and I have accumulated in our years of church planting. We planted Central City Church together. After five years of pastoring together, she moved on and eventually planted Open Church, a network of microchurches. Applying the principles we learned from Central City, a church centered on a Sunday experience in a predominately white, wealthy, inner suburb, to Open Church, a church without a Sunday experience, centered around those in recovery or living on the margins, has forced us to unpack the deeper principles of church planting as they apply to diverse expressions of faith.

The book is divided into two parts: "Getting Started" and "Preparing to Launch." The first part focuses on preliminary steps, including self-reflection on calling and motivation, defining the vision and mission, and creating a ministry action plan. It also emphasizes the importance of partnerships with parent churches and how to incorporate prayer into the church planting process. The second part is dedicated to launching the church, covering topics such as building a launch team, recruiting leaders, community organizing, marketing, and preparing for the initial launch event. It is designed to be adaptable, offering strategies not just for churches that launch with weekly worship services but for non-traditional gatherings or fresh expressions. The theology and advice are rooted in fostering authentic relationships and being open to new ideas while remaining rooted in biblical principles.

Throughout the handbook, you'll find guidance in creating a sustainable, generous, and inclusive faith community that will make the world a better place. Along with stories and advice, the book comes with dozens of templates, samples, and other resources to use along the way.

Church Planter's Toolkit

Along with this book, take advantage of the toolkit that comes with this book. There are samples, assessments, tools, and more available at churchplantershandbook.org. These resources are cataloged by the chapters in this book. After each chapter, there is a list of resources to help you implement what you've read. To access the Church Planter's Toolkit, enter the passcode found on page 207 of this book.

Generosity & Stewardship

After much consideration, it was decided not to have a chapter on generosity. This isn't because it's not important, but because it's too important. The best way to fund a church plant and build towards sustainability is to **incorporate generosity into every facet of the process.** As such, you can find "Growing Generous Givers" tips throughout the book, offering ideas and advice for how each chapter relates to fundraising. You can also go to the Church Planters' Toolkit to find resources related to fundraising and financial systems:

- Sample Church Plant Budgets by Year
- Giving Talk Guide for Churches
- Key Components for a One-Pager
- Sustainability Audit
- Launch Team Covenant

Part 1

Getting Started

Chapter 1

Reasons to Plant a Church (and Reasons Not To)

Countless church plants rise and fall for various reasons. Examining the motivations behind a church plant is one of the most important things to consider in determining its sustainability. While there are countless factors used to determine the viability of a new church, including funding, location, experience, and giftedness, none is as pervasive as the motivations that drive each of these factors. Churches founded on unhealthy motivations run the risk of closing, or worse, perpetuating unhealthy expressions of our faith.

This is not a binary conversation of good versus evil. Everyone has a mixture of healthy and unhealthy motivations. The goal here isn't to make you feel bad about one and good about the other. Or to count them up and see if your healthy motivations outnumber the unhealthy ones. Motivations aren't binary; they don't fit into simple categories. Motivation is a spectrum and there are good and bad and healthy and unhealthy motivations all along the spectrum.

The goal in this chapter is to help leaders come to terms with their motivations, to better understand the driving forces, unpack them, and learn how to lean into the motivations that will bring about the healthiest forms of church.

First, let's set the bar for success. A healthy, *successful* church plant is a church that is doing good in the world in a *sustainable* way. You can come up with your own definition for succuss, and many people have, but one thing every definition of success needs to include is some kind of metric for *sustainability*. This goes beyond financial sustainability. A church must become something that operates year after year, which means a healthy church requires healthy leaders and a healthy community. No amount of funding can replace the inner work needed in the life of the church planter. A well-funded church will close if the church planter becomes burnt out, disenfranchised, disillusioned, or hurt along the way. In other words, a sustainable church is both financially *and* emotionally sustainable. A large church that perpetuates hate is less successful than an inclusive house church impacting their neighborhood. Positive impact done in a sustainable way is the best definition for success.

A close examination of motivations will go a long way towards helping leaders set realistic goals and expectations, diminishing the chances of burnout. You might consider skipping this part to get to the more practical parts of church planting. Don't. There is nothing more practical than the motivation that drives us. You can't lead with a compelling vision when your motivation is unclear, or worse, misplaced.

Motivation is personal, and even the healthiest motivations can become unhealthy. For example, a call from God to plant a church is a good motivation, yet people have claimed a call from God to justify doing all kinds of horrible things. One doesn't disqualify the other. This isn't a checklist but a conversation, and through the conversation, you will uncover the tools you can use for your own self-discovery and reflection.

One of the best ways to determine the health of a motivation is by the fruit it produces in your life and in the community. If you measure the success of a motivation by the metrics we use in the church, you might lean into motivations that help drive attendance or financial success. But measuring success on church attendance or money can be very unhealthy—it can create anxiety, make you feel like a failure, and cause you to freeze up and stop leading. For some, it might be life-giving, and if that's true, then run with it. The real gauge is if it produces positive results in your life and in the life of your community. When you lean into a particular motivation, are you experiencing more peace, patience, kindness, self-control, goodness, joy? Healthy motivations will propel you forward, give you energy, teach contentment, sustain you during times of conflict and struggle, and help you feel good about what you accomplish. Healthy motivations will make your life more meaningful.

Unhealthy motivations will rob you of energy, create the highest highs and the lowest lows, make you want to quit and throw in the towel, and ultimately distract you from your goals. Unhealthy motivations will cause anxiety, depression, discouragement, and in general, ruin the quality of your life.

Before planting and at every step of the process, set aside time to reflect on your motivations.

You can do this carefully and strategically. Take a moment and breathe deeply. Remove yourself from distractions. Find a quiet, calming place. Set aside time. Begin this process with a prayer or setting an intention. *What do you hope to get out of this time of soul searching?*

You might consider offering up the prayer of Psalm 139:

> Search me, God, and know my heart;
> test me and know my anxious thoughts.
> See if there is any offensive way in me,
> and lead me in the way everlasting.
> (Psalm 139:23-24 NIV)

Then end this time in a similar way. Breathe, reflect, and set your intention going forward. This spiritual practice of setting an intention can help these conversations remain manageable, and their impact, lasting.

We're going to look at both, but to start, let's look at some unhealthy motivations for starting a new church.

Unhealthy Motivation #1: Unresolved Church Hurt

Have you been hurt by the church? Many people have, and many churches are now connecting with, caring for, and helping bring healing to countless people hurt by churches, maybe including the church where you're now serving. Reaching people hurt by the church is a great driving force. Having said that, in those seasons where you're sitting *in your own hurt*, it's not the healthiest driving force. Planting a church that reaches people who have been hurt is great. Planting a church *out of your own hurt and bitterness* before you've had time to heal a little, could be problematic.

Jay experienced immense pain at the hands of a pastor. There was corruption and secrecy and a community that he cared about was ultimately closed. This left a huge wound in his heart. Less than two months later, he shared with the world that he was starting a new church.

It's exciting anytime someone wants to plant a church, and this was no exception. But it'd be wise for Jay to consider a few questions first. *Why are you planting a church? Is it to reach new people? Is it to do church differently? Or is it because you're angry at your old church and so hurt that you're ruminating and daydreaming of a church plant as a way to cope?*

Can you plant a church immediately after being hurt by one? Sure. With God, anything is possible. And let's be careful not to say, "That's not how it's done!" At the same time, be sure to reflect on your motivations. To ponder: What is the driving force?

And here's why. If you're mad at the church and that's a main driving force, you might find your motivation wane. The simple truth is that you won't always be angry. You won't always be angry at that church who hurt you or the pastor who treated you with disrespect, or that leader who forced their way. Those feelings of pain are real, but they won't last forever (and if they do, we have a bigger problem). So, if you're planting a church to prove them wrong, or to cope with it, what will be your motivation when you've healed from that pain? Is there anything under that pain that is more lasting?

Healthy motivations last. They last because they come from places of health and growth. Unhealthy motivations, like unhealthy organisms, grow weaker over time, and will eventually die—or kill their host, which has the same result. Healthy motivations, like healthy organisms, grow and thrive and will live much longer than sick ones.

If you've been hurt by the church, you have a story and experience that could help a lot of people. We need the church you're about to plant. Don't give up. But there's a difference between planting out of your *hurt* versus planting out of your *healing*.

How do you tell if your motivation is for hurt or healing? The answer might sound counter intuitive. Trauma and pain push people to prove themselves, forcing them to work harder than is necessary, finding it hard to rest, or turn off, or find a work-life balance. Joanne Frederick, LCPC, licensed clinical professional counselor based in Washington, DC, explains it like this:

> When we are stuck in a less-than-ideal situation, our bodies will react instantly based on the previous trauma we are or have been experiencing. If someone with trauma finds themselves in a situation similar to what they were doing when the trauma occurred, they will preemptively push themselves to overcome the issue so that they will not have to relive the problem.[1]

As a result, those motivated from hurt will work harder and longer than those motivated from healing. And while this might sound perfect for a church planter, it is not sustainable.

One of the signs that you're healing is that your motivation can feel less intense. As Dr. Frederick explains, "When a person begins to heal from their trauma, they will start to allow themselves more room to relax."

Motivation from healing feels less urgent, severe, and intense, and outlasts motivation from trauma. It's the classic story of the tortoise and the hare. The hare might be quicker, but in the end, it's the slow, steady progress of the tortoise that wins the race. Trauma tries to race to the finish line but rarely has the strength to finish a short race before crashing and burning. Healing can run a marathon and get up the next day to play a round of golf.

Reflection

- Have you been hurt by the church? Does this drive an unhealthy urgency in church planting?
- Do you find it easy to take time off, put work down, or relax?
- Where are you on your journey of healing? What next steps are you going to take to have a healthier work and life balance?

Chapter 1

Unhealthy Motivation #2: Beat the Competition

The United Methodist denomination has gone through a schism. This means that quite a few churches in the United States are no longer United Methodist. Considering the presence of an existing church is one of the major deterrents to denominational church planting, the lack of churches in otherwise thriving communities is now driving the conversation, on both sides of the schism. There are multiple examples where a church left or stayed, and the competing denomination quickly worked up plans to plant a replacement.

This drive behind church planting is concerning. It would be great to plant a church to reach people the opposing churches are going to push away, but it could be just as easy to plant a church in these communities to *compete* with the churches that left—to show them "*We can do it too*!" Planting a church out of competition or out of spite sets the wrong tone for a new congregation.

This isn't just true for denominations. Wanting to win is a core human desire, and it can be a powerful motivation for a lot of things. Church planting, or church leadership in general, is riddled with opportunities to compare and compete. When pastors introduce themselves, the number one question they get around to asking is "How many people do you have in attendance?" or "What size is your church?"

There is a major flaw in this thinking. Competition is rooted in a scarcity mindset. Competition implies that there are only so many prizes to go around, and you either win one or don't. When we give into the temptation to view church as a competition, we forget that God does not operate out of our scarcity mindset. It's not like there's only so many people in the world, and God's going to give a prize to the church that wins over the most. The same is true for funding, resources, leaders—anything you measure or track. In God's economy of abundance, there is more than enough to go around. There's no need to compete.

A church planter shared their vision for launching a new church in a small community to a room full of life-long United Methodists. An older woman interrupted and asked the church planter, "There are already three United Methodist Churches in the area. Are you saying you're going to start a fourth?"

This question is dripping with scarcity mindset and fear of competition.

The church planter smiled, and said, "Or five or six… how many United Methodist Churches are too many?"

That's a good question: When should we stop planting new churches? If we stopped seeing new churches as competitors and started to see them as another expression of God's inclusive love, it becomes easier to answer. At what point should we stop inviting people into communities of inclusive love?

Competition isn't always a bad thing. A Harvard Business Review article explored the differences between good and bad competition.

> What distinguishes competitions that unleash creativity from competitions that cause unethical behaviors? It depends on how the competition makes employees feel.
>
> Some competitions elicit fear and anxiety, because they focus employees on the threat of being laid off, losing income, or being publicly humiliated. Other competitions focus employees on winning a coveted bonus or public recognition, which create arousal but make people feel anticipation and excitement.[2]

Competition rooted in failure creates anxiety and fear. Competition rooted in positivity or reward can be motivating for some people. If you find competition a positive force in your life and it motivates you, then lean into it.

The difference between good and bad competition has more to do with the state of the one participating and can be separated with a simple question: If you lose this competition, will you be, ok? Will things be fine? If you lose this competition, will you still consider yourself successful? Competition that makes someone feel as if they are a failure if they lose, is unhealthy. Competition that doesn't threaten one's belonging and security and is just for fun, is fine. Thinking about it this way, you can decide for yourself if your motivation is healthy or unhealthy.

If you struggle with being too competitive, the easiest way to quench it is to consciously choose to celebrate other people's success. When you hear of a church doing something well, give thanks to God for that. Be happy for them. Choosing to celebrate other people's success helps your brain remember that this isn't a competition. In God's grace, we're all winners already.

Reflection

- Do you find it easy to compare your success or your church's success to other churches?
- What does "winning" look like for you in a church plant?
- When you see or hear of a church like yours doing better at something, whether that be fundraising, reaching people, music, children's ministry, etc., do you find it easy or difficult to celebrate their success?
- Do you tend to assume there's only so much to go around and thus feel the need to go after whatever you can get your hands on? Or do you believe that there's more than enough to go around, and that God will provide for you and other churches, equally?

Unhealthy Motivation #3: Success and Notoriety

Striving after notoriety is not looked upon kindly by scripture. Going back to Genesis 1–11, we see the story of God's creation climax with the people coming together to build a tower that would reach into the heavens. They wanted to gather more people than anyone else in a tower larger than any other before it. The desire to build the largest building—and put your name on it—is as primal as they come. Rarely do people praise historic temples, in any faith, for their humility or small stature.

Consider the seven wonders of the ancient world. More than half of these were built for religious purposes: The Mayan pyramid was used for religious rituals, Christ the Redeemer in Rio de Janeiro is obvious, the Taj Mahal was built as a memorial for an emperor's wife and includes Islamic promises of the afterlife carved into the marble, and the original purpose of Machu Picchu is unknown, but most of the theories are rooted in religious practice. If you dig even deeper, the only one of the modern seven wonders of the world that wasn't at some point used for religious purposes is the Great Wall of China. There's something in us humans—especially religious humans—that wants to create something big and beautiful for our gods. While this is not inherently bad, it is unhealthy if done from the wrong motivation.

The same could be said of the original temple in Jerusalem, as Isaiah 66:1 once said, "Heaven is my throne, and **earth is my footstool**. So where could you build a house for me." This might be why John declares in his vision in Revelation that he sees no temple (Revelation 22:21). The same was true during the time of the Tower of Babel. God is not pleased with the humans' desire to conquer, compete, compare, or rule. God tried to put an end to that in Genesis 11, but we've been falling into the same trap ever since.

When God's Spirit fell on the people at Pentecost it was meant to be a great reversal of the Tower of Babel. Instead of building a tower that would reach the heavens, God would send God's Spirit to bring heaven to earth. Instead of forcing everyone to speak the same language and embrace the same culture, the Spirit communicated to people in their own language (Acts 2:8-12). Instead of building a mega-church in Jerusalem, the Spirit dispersed the people, sending them all over the Roman Empire (Acts 1:8). The story of Pentecost, the birthday of the church, shows us that God is not interested in the great institutions we humans conjure up. God is interested in a community that is authentically dispersed.

Striving to be the best, strongest, most influential is natural, but it's not a motivation we should feed. It does not reflect the upside-down kingdom Jesus came to establish. As Jesus said, "You are not to be like that. Instead, the greatest among you should be like the youngest, and the one who rules like the one who serves" (Luke 22:25-27).

This one hits a little too close to home for me. I'd be lying if I didn't set out to plant a church with a little bit of hope that I might plant the "next big thing." I wanted to *wow* and impress my denominational leaders and gain the notoriety I see other pastors have. When we launched with 100 people and a year later had a service with only 40 in attendance—well, my dreams of being the "next big thing" came crashing down. This led me on a journey of self-discovery, and I had to do the hard work of redefining what success looks like.

Whether you are seen as successful, feel successful, or feel like a failure (or all three at different times, which is how most people experience it), your relationship with notoriety and recognition is a necessary part of spiritual growth. We all must do the hard work of coming to terms with our definition of success.

Reflection

- How do you define success?
- What milestones have you set that are equally difficult while still attainable given your resources, gifts, and calling?

Unhealthy Motivation #4: To Save the Church

The church is declining in America. Established congregations are getting older and smaller. The church needs something new, but if not carefully considered, this could become an unhealthy motivation. Many established church pastors and leaders talk about church planting (or really any church renewal tool) as some kind of *savior*. They are reaching for something—anything—to give them hope.

That is why this needs to be said—and read it a couple of times before moving on: *We shouldn't plant churches to save the church.*

This is important to understand in a couple of ways.

First, it's not our job. The church belongs to God, and our local congregations and church plants are just a small part of God's plan in this world. Church planting can't save the church because church planting isn't the Savior. Jesus has that more than covered. Whatever happens to the church is out of our hands. It's above our paygrade. It's more than we can take on. Trying to plant churches to save the church forces us to take on a motivation and drive that is more than we are asked to carry. God doesn't need us to be God. God wants us to be the individual people God created us to be. *Small, little humans with limited time and resources.* This might be discouraging, but there is great relief in knowing that *it's ok to be human.* God will take care of the Church and all you need to do is to commit to play your part in it.

Second, a new church plant doesn't work to save a declining church. If a church is declining, it's declining for a reason. It might be a good idea to plant a new church to reach the neighborhood but if its mission is to save the established church next door, it will fail. The established congregation is going to continue, as it has, until it can't. A new church needs to live its own life cycle and not be expected to keep a dying church alive.

Life and death are necessary parts of this world, and essential to our theology. Things are born and things die, and as people of faith, we believe things can rise again. This cycle of life, death and resurrection is everything to us. This does not mean we shouldn't mourn the things we've lost, or take time to grieve, but we also should not pretend like everything is going to last forever. We should respect churches wherever they are in their life-journey and not expect them to be something they aren't.

Everything has its season.

Think of it this way. If your grandmother, at the age of 99, ended up in hospice, it would be wildly inappropriate to ask her to join the launch team for a new church. Can you imagine trying to learn a bunch of new contemporary songs and get up and go out and reach new people? If she doesn't, the church is going to die! So now your grandmother, nearing the end of her life, has to finish her time at church feeling responsible for the future of the church. Does that seem loving and kind to you? Is that what God meant when God said care for the elderly? Your grandmother doesn't need a church planter; she needs a chaplain. Anything else would be unloving.

Now, imagine your daughter is recently married and becomes pregnant, and everyone is so excited, including you! So, you share with your daughter, *"Dear, I'm so glad you're having a baby, cause as you know your grandmother isn't going to live much longer and we really need a new child to replace her."*

Please don't ever say this.

In the grand scheme of things, this is how death and life works—new children are born and our elderly pass away—but just because it's *true* doesn't mean *it needs to be said.* All this does is pit the grandmother's life against the birth of her great grandchild. Don't plant new churches to replace the old; plant new churches because you are excited about bringing something new into the world.

This kind of conversation and attitude plays out far too often between church plants and legacy congregations. When we think of the new as a replacement for the old, we pit one against the other. By doing so, we have robbed each of the chance to love, care, support, and get to know the other. Instead of thinking of new churches as replacements for old churches, think of new churches as grandchildren you love. You might not always understand them, but you can love them all the same.

Reflection

- Have you ever been a part of a church in the second half of its life? Have you ever been a part of a church that has closed?
- What experiences have you had with well-established churches?
- Do you feel pressure to launch a church in order to save an established congregation or denomination or the Church at large? If so, how are you able to process these expectations in a healthy way?

Unhealthy Motivation #5: To Reproduce Your Preferences

If you're a part of a church and that church has made a huge impact on your life and the life of your family and friends, and you want to see more churches like your church and give people more experiences like your experience, then it's only fair to try and duplicate what you love.

This isn't inherently bad, but it does come with a caution.

Most of what you love about church is a personal preference.

Take a second and ponder this. It's a true statement and needs to be fully considered.

Most of what you love about a church is a personal preference. Not all personal preferences need to be duplicated. The experience you had that you want to duplicate might not work for a different culture, whether that be generational, racial, ethnic, or socio-political. At worst, this motivation can border on colonization, if not carefully evaluated. It's possible to move to a different country (or different neighborhood) with sincere intentions to give people something you have found wildly meaningful, rooted in your personal preferences and cultural heritage, aiming to convince your neighbors to conform to your view of church. For example, if you love traditional worship, wearing a suit and tie, having the pastor in a robe, and sitting on a traditional church committee—that's great! But you need to realize that other people might not attend your church, including many young people. You don't have to be upset by that. People are allowed to like different things.

A church plant launched a few years ago as a stereotypical evangelical, contemporary church. They had a modern name, a professional logo, and upbeat worship. Yet, for whatever reason, many ex-Catholics and Lutherans were visiting and attending. The church was reaching people who were no longer attending church but were raised in very traditional settings. Because they understood and processed their cultural assumptions, this church plant was able to pivot. Now, they have a band and contemporary worship, but they also take time to read the creeds, offer a prayer of confession, and have a liturgist.

Our faith can thrive in all kinds of practices and customs. In fact, Christianity is one of the few world religions that has seen the center of faith shift over time. If you lay out a map and chart where the majority of people of a particular faith live and worship, it tends to decrease and spread out from that center. This is often called the diaspora—the faith is rooted in one place, but people practice in a multitude of places. Unlike most other world religions, our faith's center has shifted over time. What started as a religion rooted in the Middle East shifted its center to Europe, and then, over time, the center moved to America. Now, we see it moving to the southern hemisphere, Africa, and Southeast Asia. Most other religions are often geographically centered around the location of their founder. Not Christianity. It has historically taken on the culture and values of its host countries and spread like wildfire. While this doesn't always produce positive results (I'm looking at you, Christian nationalism), it is a testimony to the flexibility and adaptability of our faith. Our faith can live in a myriad of cultures and be expressed in a variety of personal preferences.

As a church planter, you need to be aware of your cultural assumptions and try not to turn these into non-negotiables. This includes your assumptions about worship styles, polity, and membership expectations. To expect others who are different from you to find your cultural expression of Christianity meaningful is unhealthy and rooted in toxic, authoritarian theology.

It's healthy to want people to have a similar experience as you, but depending on the situation, you might have to learn culturally and contextually appropriate ways to live it out. The goal isn't to get someone to like traditional worship, or worship in the round, or decentralized leadership, or any other element of church and community diversity, but to help someone experience God in a culturally relevant way, whether that be through traditional worship, a Bible study at a local brewery, serving on a committee, or volunteering at a homeless shelter. If you love something, then it's very healthy to want to see more of it. But be careful. Be sure you're not projecting your church expectations onto those you're trying to gather.

Reflection

- Are you approaching church planting with uncovered biases and assumptions around what people want in a church?
- What time have you spent getting to know your community, engaging in cultural competency education, and dismantling the cultural expressions of your faith that might limit your ability to connect with new people?

- Consider three practices you love about church. Would you give those things up if necessary, in reaching new people? What are the underlying principles or values at work in those practices? For example, your love for traditional music points to a value that you want music that people can connect with. How might you lean into the deeper values instead of your personal preferences?

Unhealthy Motivation #6: No Other Options

Once this motivation is named, it's more embarrassing than anything. The simple truth is that some people pursue church planting because they haven't been able to pastor in an established church. A pastor might leave a toxic church, and since they have nowhere to go, they try church planting. In most cases, nothing comes of the church plant, and in the process, significant denominational funding can be wasted. It's possible that a church planter might struggle in an established church or get bored or discouraged, and once they experience the joys of church planting, they come alive. It's true, a church planter might struggle in a traditional church, but the opposite isn't equally true. Just because someone struggles in a traditional church doesn't mean they are a church planter. There has to be another reason for giving your life to starting a church than simply running out of options.

Let's look at some of these reasons.

Healthy Motivation #1: Provide Space for New People, New Generations, and New Ideas

New churches are the best way for people disconnected from church to find a place to belong. A small group at an established church was asked if they would be open to including some new people into the group. They were friendly and supportive and yet, they weren't sure they wanted to open it up to new people. They explained that the group had been meeting for so long, that they had countless inside jokes and context and trust, that it would be hard including a new person. Their self-awareness is commendable. At least they were honest. More churches should be this self-aware. The simple truth is, it doesn't matter how nice you are, it's hard for new people to get connected in well-established communities. Not impossible, just harder.

There's nothing wrong with becoming an established church—don't forget, it's the goal! A church plant would consider itself blessed to survive the risk of its early years of launching, to become stable and established. The issue with established churches is that no matter how friendly they are, they have a way of doing things, a set of assumptions they aren't aware of that guide their decisions. They have a rich history that new people are unfamiliar with. All of these realities can make it hard for new people to break in.

The great benefit of a church plant is that everyone is new, and the history is being written in our midst.

Allyssa and I were meeting with a couple interested in joining our launch team, and they asked how things were going. We had about 50 people on our team so far. They were impressed, and then they paused. "Does that include us?" It did. They had said they were interested. They were a solid "*maybe*," so they counted. They thought it was strange that they were considered in that number with such a non-committal response, but that's the beauty of a church plant—*if you're interested, then you belong.* Come join us!

Established churches have history. Try pitching a new idea to an established church and they will likely tell you all the times they have tried something similar and why it failed. This so-called "wisdom" is often used to discourage things from changing. A church planter wishes things into existence in a world that prefers things remain the same. Anyone who does anything new will face people who tell you, "That's not how it's done." Do it anyway.

New churches can try things because they are young and naive enough not to know any better. Naïveté is a gift. It's a gift that you get at the start of something new. It's a gift of childhood, and any time something new is being born into the world, it starts as a child. That's why Jesus says the kingdom of God belongs to children—that the only way to enter the kingdom is to become a child (Matthew 18:3). If you want to try a new idea, connect with new people, gather the next generation, and explore the myriad different ways people can connect with God, church plants are a great place to do it.

Reflection

- What does it mean to you to reach and gather new people?
- Do you get excited about meeting new people looking for a church? Where do you think this excitement comes from?
- What new ideas do you hope to bring to a new church?

Healthy Motivation #2: Love of God

When we get to the crux of the matter, and all the glory and ideas and creativity and pressure are tossed aside, hopefully your motivation to plant a church is rooted in the love of God and the outpouring of that love in the world. The church—or gathering of God's people—is the primary way God is bringing God's kingdom to earth. Properly positioned as a force for good, a church makes the world a better place.

Many people in the world are fed up with the church. They see the church as a corrupt institution that protects abusers, causes harm to LGBTQ+ people, and perpetuates patriarchy. Religion has been the source of much harm in the world, and there are people who think of church in this way.

Yet, in many other ways, the church has made the world a better place. The church founded most of the western institutes for higher education, most ministries to the hurting and poor are led by religious people from a variety of faith traditions, and most hospitals are tied to religious traditions. The church *can be* a positive force in the world, and given the church's track record and national landscape, a church planter needs to be prepared to explain to someone why planting a church will make the world a better place.

This is a great way to test your motives. Imagine talking to someone who sees religions as a source of all the bad in the world. When you talk to them, they bring up the crusades, the holy wars, the protection of abusers and pedophiles, the harm caused to LGBTQ+ people, the way the church has been co-opted by political parties and white nationalists, and how the church has used the fear of hell to control and scare people. Imagine you're talking to someone like that, and you're going to explain *why* you're starting a new church. In this scenario, there are certain motivations that will only strengthen their case. If you're doing it only because your denomination has asked you to, that only further convinces them of the power religious institutions have over people. If you tell them it's because you want people to not end up in hell, that only confirms their assumptions about how the church uses hell to persuade people into good behavior. If you tell them it's because your city is evil and you believe God wants to save it, that only confirms their assumptions that you are going to look down and judge people. If you tell them you have the answers and you can fix what's broken in the world and only the church can help those who are hurting, that will only strengthen their assumptions about Christians having a messiah complex.

Growing Generous Givers

People are intuitive, and it seems those who have been hurt by the church or experience church trauma are especially tuned into motivation. They will sense what drives you. You won't be able to hide it. They might never be able to put words to what they are feeling or be able to name it, but they will sense it. If you haven't done the hard work of reflecting on your motivations, it can hurt your ability to ask people to give. Your request for donations is going to come from the motivations that are driving your desire to start a church. Why should someone give to help you become successful? Or to perpetuate toxic theology? Or to help you be judgmental to those living outside the church? Or any other less-than-noble reason? People give because they want to see good things happen in the world. Let this be your motivation for planting a church and you will be able to sincerely and with integrity ask people to give for the same reason.

None of these are worthwhile, long-lasting motivations. On the other hand, If you respond to the question "Why plant a church when religion causes harm?" by talking about how you personally love the way of Jesus and therefore value living in a community with people from all walks of life because you can learn from what others have to offer and want to create a safe place to heal from harm by using the community's collective power to bring about goodness—well, that doesn't sound so bad. Plant a church rooted in Jesus's love. Plant a church because you believe it will make the world a better place and be prepared to explain why.

Healthy Motivation #3: Call of God

Apostle Niki Hampton, a fellow church planter, once told me, "Church planting can be a great experience, *if you are called to it.*" She has always been good at distilling wisdom into simple, profound proverbs. But there was a tone in her voice and a sense of peace in her presence—as if she might be reflecting on all those who went in for the wrong reasons—as if she knew firsthand the difficulty of starting something new, but how none of that matters if you were able to experience the call of God. She spoke as if she took comfort in knowing that God was *with* her and *for* her.

God wants us to start new churches. A simple reflection of scripture and the New Testament will provide ample evidence. The question becomes: Are *you* called to plant a church? That is a harder question to answer.

Each story and journey to church planting is different. Yet, they often have something in common. Most people who plant a church experience some kind of calling. Having a calling pushes people to do hard things. Church planters often want to quit—and for the ones that don't, they can tell you a story where they came close. In every instance, the thing that keeps church planters going is a drive in their soul, a push that is hard to explain. *How could I do anything else?* It's like what Peter said when Jesus asked the disciples if they wanted to quit following him: *"Where would we go?"* (John 6:68).

If you're wondering if you're called, and you're not sure, try and do something else. Play the idea out in your head and ask yourself how you feel. Could you live with yourself? Could you make it work? Would you be happy? Or would you feel a little like Jonah running from Nineveh? If you were told that you didn't *have* to plant a church, would you be *relieved* or *anxious*?

When the dust settles and you are no longer sad, depressed, hurting, or angry, do you want to keep doing it? If so, that's what makes it a calling. A calling remains, even when your motivation shifts and moves. A calling doesn't require any effort to keep alive. You can leave it behind, throw it away, step on it, get mad at it, and when everything calms back down and you ask yourself what you want to do, the calling pops up, like it had been there the whole time just waiting for you to get over yourself.

The best part of a calling is that it can eclipse our unhealthy motivations. Do you think Jonah had the right motivation when he finally made his way to Nineveh? He went begrudgingly, with a racist fear of outsiders. Yet, God used him anyway. It's interesting when you think about it. In that story, Jonah was the only one to suffer from his unhealthy motivation. He went to Nineveh only after being forced to and preached the message God had given to him. He was eventually faithful, and the people turned their lives around. They were changed for the better, but not Jonah. His life suffered from his hardened heart. Jonah ends up on a hill, mad at God, pouting and frustrated. His faithfulness, even if forced, changed the lives of people, but his less-than-ideal motivations made his *own life* horrible. This is one of the main reasons to consider your motivations. It's for your own benefit, so that you don't end up on a hill, pouting and mad. It doesn't matter how good of a pastor you are, if you go in with the wrong expectations or motivations, unwilling to reflect or address them, you will end up just like Jonah: angry, sad, depressed, and mad at God.

God can use you regardless of what drives you, but some things will bring you life and working through your less-than-ideal motivations can help you better enjoy the fruit of your faithfulness. Thinking through our motivations is important for personal growth, but that says nothing about our worthiness or calling. God calls and uses imperfect people. So, let's reflect and grow, while also giving ourselves grace and patience.

Reflection

- How have you experienced a call to church planting?
- In what ways has this call been confirmed by others?
- In what ways have people failed to see this call, and how have you processed these perspectives?
- If you were to give up church planting right now, would you be relieved or anxious?
- What fruit do you have from starting new things in the past?

A Jonah Story

Sara never wanted to be a church planter.

She is an open-minded, inclusive pastor serving in a rural suburban, conservative world. Her church home decided to disaffiliate from the United Methodist Church. This is where she had baptized her kids and where she first heard her call to ministry. The conference had seen the writing on the wall for years, so they asked her to consider starting a church. She made it clear she wasn't interested. She never wanted to be a church planter!

It was her husband that invited her to reconsider. You need to know, he doesn't (often) weigh in on many spiritual matters. It's all sports or *Star Wars* for him. He's not going around quoting scripture. He left that to his wife and pastor. This made his next comment all the starker. "Sara, a whale's gonna swallow you up and spit you right back out here in our town where you don't want to plant!"

She looked at him, dumbfounded. "Did you just make a biblical reference?" Her husband didn't know that she recently registered for a retreat based on Jonah, titled "Belly of the Whale Retreat."

Even with all of this, she had her hesitations. When her District Superintendent called asking her to consider planting a church, Sara quickly gave him all the reasons why it was a bad idea. This was her hometown; these were her friends—she couldn't be a pastor to her best friends! Also, it would be better to have a guy do it—that would go over more smoothly in the area. She gave him every possible reason for it being a bad idea. Then, before hanging up, she told him what her husband had said about Jonah. The District Superintendent laughed way too hard for way too long, and then added, "What I'm hearing is that you're not saying *no*."

Sara's summer was full of prayer and conversations and wrestling with lots of fear. Sara attended that retreat focused on the story of Jonah. In those same days her home church held a vote to disaffiliate from the UMC.

Later that summer, Sara went on vacation with her family. With all these thoughts of calling and whales fresh on her mind, she walked the beaches along Oak Island, North Carolina. Throughout the area, there were countless warning signs for rip tides. She'd read these signs, as she pondered what she might do next in life and ministry. The image of a riptide began to haunt her. A riptide is a powerful force that seizes the ocean's surface, dragging swimmers unexpectedly away from shore with a relentless pull. The only way to get out of a riptide is to allow the tide to pull you out into deeper water and trust that help will come. That's when she realized, "Out in these deeper waters, it's not about swimming harder or trying with more strength," explained Sara, "It's about going with the flow and keeping your eyes on the shore, trusting that hope will come." She paused and then looked back up. "And with that, I agreed to plant a church."

She realized it was about trust—trusting God with each step, trusting God with the community, trusting and going with the flow, going deeper—keeping her eyes on Christ and following the call where it leads.

"It has led to a healing space," she said, "a difficult space, a safe but sometimes uncomfortable space, a place where we set up chairs every week, going with the flow of the Holy Spirit, and trust that God will be with us..."

Motivation Reflections

Consider spending time with these questions before moving forward with church planting:

1. Why do you want to plant a church? What motivates you? Consider coming up with a list of all the reasons you want to plant a church—the healthy and maybe not-so-healthy motivations. Consider your top two healthy motivations in planting a church and then consider your top two unhealthy motivations.
    a. Healthy Motivations:
        i. ____________________________
        ii. ____________________________
    b. Unhealthy motivations:
        i. ____________________________
        ii. ____________________________
2. What are some things you can do to feed your healthy motivations? How can you invest in these motivations?
3. What are some things you can do to better understand and process your unhealthy motivations? How can you ensure they won't derail your goals and vision?

Church Planter's Toolkit

Go to churchplantershandbook.org to access the following resources related to this chapter:

- **Motivation Reflection Guide**: Use this collection of questions to work through your discernment in church planting.
- **The Entrepreneur Assessment**: This assessment is great for anyone who's thinking about starting something from scratch, whether that's a new church, nonprofit, or social enterprise. It only takes 10-15 minutes, and when you're done, it provides custom recommendations that will help you become the best entrepreneur you can be.

To access the Church Planter's Toolkit at churchplantershandbook.org, enter this passcode: PLANT!TOOLS

Chapter 2

Vision & Mission

In the opening scene of Ridley Scott's *Gladiator*, Marcus Aurelius pulls Maximus aside and begins to reminisce about the origins of Rome. When you're a part of starting something new, and you get to see it become something great, it's hard not to reflect on such origins. Filled with these thoughts, he looks at Maximus, and declares, "There was once a dream that was Rome. You could only whisper it. Anything more than a whisper and it would vanish."

I think of this line often. When starting something new, the first glimpse of a vision is fragile. The visionary can only see small parts of it—like a blurry and out-of-focus reflection. At this stage, if shared with the wrong person too soon, the vision could get squashed before it has a chance to grow into something beautiful.

Visions start out fragile, but they don't stay that way.

Vision is like a seed. Seeds are small and easily lost. Yet, when they are planted, and cared for, they grow into something wonderful. Remember that seeds don't look anything like the plants they grow into. You might have a vision for a new church, and you work hard to prepare the soil and plant the ideas. Prayer is poured over this vision like water, and the vision grows, only to find it no longer looks quite like you thought it would. If you think of a vision as a seed, take comfort in knowing that it's doing exactly what it was designed to do. A seed can't stay a seed if it wants to grow. It has to change into something new.

Like seeds, the more beautiful the plant, the more temperamental the seed. Weeds are easy to grow, but have you ever tried to grow an orchid?

When you grow an orchid from a seed, it requires years of patience and care before you ever see a leaf, and even longer before it blooms. Healthy, diverse church plants are like orchids.

This has quite a few ramifications. For example, it's best to have a vision that isn't tied to specific programs or strategies. You might have a vision of a church with life-changing small groups that meet in people's homes, only to find now you have small groups that meet less often and hardly ever in people's homes. This is the difference between a vision and a strategy. The vision, it turned out, wasn't to have life-changing small groups that meet in people's homes. The vision was to help people find community and that, in practicing relational excellence, they might grow in their love of God and others. While the original strategy was to have weekly small groups in people's homes, the *strategy* changed, but the *vision* remained the same.

The same could be said for nearly every part of your original plan. The seeds you plant have to grow into something different than you expect.

A good vision survives the test of time. The strategy, theology, and programs implemented in churches can change wildly over the years, but much of God's first vision has a way of sticking around, through the ups and downs of ministry. If you have a vision of the church that has stuck with you over the years, lean into it. If it's stuck with you this long, then it's more likely to stick with you through the difficulty of planting a church.

Mission and Vision Statements (And How to Communicate Them)

There's a difference between a vision and a vision *statement*. A vision is the picture of what could be, and the vision statement is an imperfect way of describing this picture. No matter how good your vision statement ends up being, it will always be an inadequate picture of what God has called you to do.

The vision—the big picture God has given you—is like the painting of *Mona Lisa* and the vision statement is one sentence describing the painting: a woman, sitting in a pastoral setting, with her hands crossed. Be honest, does this statement accurately describe Mona Lisa? *Yes*. But, by itself, does it do the painting justice? *Not even close*. No one will line up to see a painting based on this statement, alone. There are a million different ways to describe the *Mona Lisa*, which is to say, statements about your vision will change over time, but the vision remains, becoming clear over time. It is as if you only got a glimpse of the vision and had to craft a vision statement from that little glimpse, but then you get another glimpse, and you can see more of it this time, and then something else happens, and you get another glimpse of what God is calling you to do. As this happens, the vision becomes clearer and your ability to communicate it is better.

Or as Paul says in 1 Corinthians: "For now we see only a reflection as in a mirror; then we shall see face to face. Now I know in part; then I shall know fully, even as I am fully known" (1 Corinthians 13:12).

Vision and mission statements, pitches, and vision stories are all working towards the common goal of bringing people face to face with an intangible vision God has given you. With this in mind, let's walk through how to create practical vision and mission statements. But first, definitions.

> **Mission statement:** To describe succinctly what it is you hope to *do* or who you want to *be.*
>
> **Vision Statement:** To describe succinctly how the world or your community will be *different* if you were able to accomplish your mission.

Consider this in the context of a story like *Lord of the Rings*. The story begins with a simple mission. A group from Middle-earth form a fellowship to take the ring from the Shire to Mount Doom to destroy it. That's the mission—*what they are trying to do*—and it could easily be re-written to become the fellowship's mission statement.

"Form a fellowship to destroy the ring and save Middle-earth." A simple mission statement.

On the other hand, the vision statement, or what they hope to accomplish through this mission, describes all the ways they can imagine how Middle-earth would be different if they were successful in accomplishing it.

A mission statement drives you to action, and a vision statement paints the picture of what it will look like when you're successful.

When drafting a vision and mission statement, set aside only an appropriate amount of time for this. There are far more important things to occupy your time than crafting the perfect mission and vision statements. The goal isn't to create the perfect statement, but to create clarity about what you hope to do. You need multiple ways to share and explain it to others. The goal is effective communication, not a well-written sentence.

Start big and narrow it down. Write out everything—this should be more than one page of notes. Include your hopes for worship, discipleship, mission, community, leadership, etc. Don't hold back. This is a place to include everything, even if it's not helpful. Spend a few days or weeks adding to this document as new ideas come. When you're ready, read over the document.

Highlight or underline key words, phrases, or ideas. You're looking for the big ideas and trends. Once you have these big ideas, trends, and key words, draft them into a simple mission statement.

Next, move on to the vision statement. What do you hope to accomplish as a new church? And how will your community, neighborhood, or city be different because of it? If the vision is to plant a church, and the only reason you can come up with to plant a church is because you want to have *another* church, then you might be in trouble. Envisioning a world with more churches isn't a compelling image. You must dig deeper. How will the neighborhood, city, or world change because you planted a church? If you are successful in accomplishing your mission, the goals you've set out, how will your life, your people's lives, and your neighbor's lives be different?

Once you have something, start using it. You can always edit it along the way.

The Pitch

A pitch is as simple as combining your vision and mission statement with the details needed for someone to respond. In other words, the pitch is:

Chapter 2

Pitch = Vision/Mission Statement + Logistics

"Here's what we're about and here's how you can be a part of it!"

Having a short, concise description of your church is invaluable for meeting new people, building a launch team, welcoming visitors, or including the church plant in small talk. It's best to have it under 60 seconds. Whether you have a half hour, all day, or just a few moments to talk about your church plant with someone, starting with the important things in the first 60 seconds will help you better communicate the essential details and can serve as an outline for the rest of your conversation. Share your pitch first with staff or core leaders and get feedback. Then share it with every person you came across, knowing it will need to be adjusted over time. Inevitably, people will ask questions, but be grateful for the questions because they will help you see the places where a pitch is unclear or needs clarification. A pitch needs to evolve, not just because the action step will change as the launch progresses, but because people's input and feedback will help you refine it.

When you write your pitch, vision, or mission statement, you'll be tempted to think, *Is this the best pitch it can be? Would it win in a competition?* That is the wrong question to consider. A better question would be, *Does it accurately, to the best of my ability, tell people what I hope to do and how they can be involved at this moment in time?* If it's as clear as it can be, in this moment in time, then you have a pitch. From there, practice it while gauging how people respond. Do people get excited? Are people interested? Does it open the conversation up or close it down? Edit your pitch accordingly.

This is one of the great lessons in church planting and applies to more than just crafting a pitch: Don't wait until it's perfect. **Start with something imperfect and be willing to adjust.**

The church planter's best tool is iteration. It's what sets entrepreneurial endeavors apart from established organizations. Starting something new requires that you start before you're ready and adjust as you go along. Ryan Babineaux, PhD, a lecturer at Stanford and author of the book, *Fail Fast, Fail Often: How Losing Can Help You Win,* calls this "failing forward." Every part of the church plant, from your communication strategy to your discipleship plan, will have success and failures. The trick is failing *fast* and failing *forward*. You can't wait for it to be perfect. Instead, be grateful for the feedback you receive and incorporate it as quickly as you can. Always do a post-mortem on every significant interaction and event so you can adjust as you go along.

What went well, and why?

- Identify the successful aspects and what contributed to them. This helps reinforce effective strategies and strengths.

What didn't go as planned, and what can be learned from it?

- Pinpoint areas that fell short and analyze the root causes to improve for next time.

What specific adjustments should be made moving forward?

- Determine actionable steps to refine your approach, whether it's tweaking communication, preparation, or execution.

What feedback would be most useful?

- Take time, especially at the beginning, asking people to share their feedback on every aspect of the vision and strategy.

When you meet with new people, and share the big-picture vision, ask simple questions like, "What kind of church do you think this community needs?" They might have ideas that help shape how you live out your vision.

Here are a few questions worth asking members of your community and prospective launch team members. Each of these can help you bring clarity to your vision.

- What do you love about this neighborhood?
- What do you think a great church in this neighborhood might look like?

These questions, and dozens of others, can be used to get people talking, and with "ears to hear and eyes to see," you will catch glimpses of the vision that God has given them for the church.

Now, take what you hear, distill it, and incorporate it into the vision you share with others for church. A church's vision might start with the pastor, but it must include everyone's voices. Remember, you have a vision no one can see yet. It's your job to take that beautiful painting in your head and talk about it in a way that people can get glimpses and want to join.

Vision Stories

Having mission and vision statements and a clever pitch is useful, but these are just the beginning, not the end, of the journey. That's where stories come in.

Consider this example. The mission statement of the United Methodist Church is to *make disciples of Jesus Christ for the transformation of the world.* Other than being rooted in rather religious terms that unchurched people might struggle to define, it's a fine mission statement that any local church could adopt. The issue with this mission statement, as with all mission statements, is this: each one of these words and phrases recalls different ideas and stories to those who read it. What do you mean "*make disciples*?" Does this mean we are going to do door-to-door evangelism? Does this mean we will be holding Sunday school classes? Does this mean that the pastor will spend all their time caring for their congregation, helping them become better disciples? These questions could continue until we've run out of paper to write them on.

This is why mission and vision statements are inadequate by themselves.

Mission and vision statements are only anchors. They hold the ship steady, keeping it from drifting too far from its destination. They are useful, a place to pivot around. They keep things clear, but they aren't the point. A mission statement without stories to back it up is like an anchor without a ship. Only stories, told repeatedly, can help shape our understanding, expectations, and assumptions around what it means to live into that vision. This is why we have the biblical canon. Many years ago, church leaders chose which stories would be included in the Scriptures. These stories now shape how we understand what it means to be a follower of Jesus.

Let's consider another mission statement, this one from Jesus. He offered it one Saturday as he opened the scroll in the synagogue and read from Isaiah:

> The Spirit of the Lord is on me,
> because he has anointed me
> to proclaim good news to the poor.
> He has sent me to proclaim freedom for the prisoners
> and recovery of sight for the blind,
> to set the oppressed free,
> to proclaim the year of the Lord's favor. (Luke 4:18-19)

This is a great mission statement! And yet, even this mission statement could be interpreted in a dozen different ways. For example, did Jesus mean the literal poor, or simply those poor in spirit? Did Jesus mean he would release people as prisoners of sin (Galatians 3:22) or was he in the business of literally releasing people from prison (Acts 16:25-34)? These questions aren't answered in the mission statement. It's only *after* Jesus tells us parables and we read the church's collection of stories of Jesus engaging in ministry—healing the blind, loving the poor, and welcoming the stranger—that we see what this mission statement looks like when it's lived out.

Consider one more mission statement, this one for a local church: *to be an incarnational community, in the urban center, where the kingdom of God becomes tangible.* This is a fine mission statement, but what does it mean, *exactly*? And can you be sure that what you think it means is the same as the church planter who came up with it? The church planter behind this mission statement had to figure out how to tell their vision and mission through stories. Stories of how she and her neighbor found someone on the corner of their street, overdosing. They quickly administered Narcan and brought this person back to life.

Would you have guessed, from her mission statement, that "incarnational community" means giving someone who was overdosing Narcan? Either way, now that you've heard the story, you know what she means. That's the power of stories.

She went on to share a story about how in churches she has served, the pastor was asked to only preach, provide pastoral care, and lead a Bible study. She talked about how she believed the pastor should also be engaged in community development, helping people grow in their faith by loving those in the margins. How lucky would you have to be to guess that is what she meant when she said, "the kingdom of God becomes tangible"?

The simple truth is that her mission statement could have been as simple as "making disciples for the transformation of the world," or any other variation, as long as she had good stories to explain what she meant. It's only after hearing a story of her saving someone's life with Narcan or meeting and building relationships with mothers doing their best to raise their children while experiencing poverty that you realize that in this church, discipleship doesn't mean Sunday school classes.

For you, Sunday school classes might be the strategy you're going to use to make disciples. If so, then you must have some compelling stories you can tell as to *why* that's a part of your vision. Tell us about the time someone lost their husband, and the Sunday school class came around them, ensuring they never felt alone in their grief. Tell us about how that widow, years later, proudly said "that Sunday school class saved my life." Tell us the importance of community, care, and love for each other.

Whatever your vision is, show us what that looks like in a story. Usually, vision is rooted in singular moments that we hope to duplicate. We have one life-changing experience, and we hope to have more of it. We see what could be, so we build something to reflect those possibilities. If this is true for you, then you already have the stories you need. It's not until we are able to share those stories in a compelling way that those coming along with us will be able to see the vision we have of church. The goal isn't to write a novel or a sermon. We're looking for short anecdotes that can be shared briefly in conversation or before meetings.

Consider the first draft of this church planter's vision story:

> This is a place where people find practical tools to live as faithful followers of Jesus in all areas of their lives, like my friend who found a way to deal with a difficult roommate during a teaching.

There's an obvious problem with this story. It's missing all the context needed for it to be compelling. There's no beginning, middle, or end. It's unclear who the main character is: Is the main character the church or the friend? Why is dealing with a difficult roommate significant to the church's mission?

With a little bit of storytelling best practices, a story is born:

> I had the chance to preach recently to a community of people recovering from addiction, and I have to say there's no better place to preach than to a room full of people in recovery. There's something about the honesty, authenticity, and rawness that feels more like the kingdom of God than most churches I've been a part of. One time, I preached a sermon where I suggested that we can have kindness even when there isn't fondness. Like most sermons, this is one of those things I've struggled with. Needless to say, I'm not an expert, and I wasn't even sure if it was going to connect with those in the room. But afterwards, as people headed out for a smoke break, a young man came up to the front to catch me and told me this was exactly what he needed to hear. Turns out he was struggling to get along with his roommate in one of his sober living homes and he was reminded he could be kind to his roommate, even when—or especially when—they weren't getting along.
>
> Life is hard, and we're not always going to get along with everyone we come across, but we're planting a church where we can learn to be kind, no matter what. This is the kind of church we're hoping to plant.

Whether you would want to be a part of this church or not is irrelevant. This story tells you exactly what this planter means when they talk about incarnational ministry and being a tangible witness to the kingdom of God. This story could be shortened, edited, and adapted for any number of situations.

These instructions are not about creating fictional stories (although the principles work the same). It would be wildly dishonest and insincere and unethical and all around horrible to tell fictional stories of life-changing events *as if* they were real. On the other hand, sometimes we do have scenes of what we want to see happen, and sharing these can be helpful, but be sure they are presented as such. For example, you might share little anecdotes, inviting people to "imagine a church where..." If presented as an invitation to dream, and clearly not a recount of what has happened, that's fine.

> Growing Generous Givers
>
> The process we used to craft and share our vision for planting a church is exactly the same process we use when raising money. When fundraising, the request isn't to join the launch team or visit a preview service, it's to make a donation. The "ask" is different, but the process is the same. The same process can be used for giving talks, the moment before taking up an offering, membership classes, or anywhere else you're asking people to support what God is doing in your church.

Share these vision stories over and over again. Be ok with repeating yourself and running the risk of someone saying, "I've heard this story before." People close to you will need to get comfortable hearing the same stories more than once, because not only do they need to be reminded, but also those who are new or those you are meeting need to hear them too.

Take time in the next few weeks, coming up with five to ten stories that help show people what you mean by your mission and vision.

1. What does it look like for your mission and vision statements to be put into action?
2. What activities does this include and what examples of transformation do you have for these activities?
3. If you were successful and accomplished what you hoped to accomplish, what kind of stories do you hope you will be able to share?
4. What story of church do you wish you could duplicate? What made it powerful or transformative?

Write them down, editing them to be concise and on point. Share them with your team, and as always, incorporate feedback as you go along. Remind them (and yourself) what it looks like to live into the vision.

The Vision Sorting Cube

When Finn, my son, was very little, he had one of those sorting cubes, where each side of the cube had a hole that had a different shape, and then corresponding blocks that fit into these holes. The star shape fits into the star hole, the rectangle fits into the rectangle hole. The same with the circle, cross, and square.

While the vision often starts with the church planter, denominational leaders, or parent churches, it has to include the ideas of those who will help carry it out. Inviting people to speak into a vision is a lot like figuring out what blocks fit into which slots in my son's sorting cube.

Leaders can fall prey to seeing their vision as an immovable document and only those willing to fall under their authority can belong to the church. "We do worship, mission, and discipleship, and these are immovable and solid, unable to be changed. We're going to do x, y, and z this way and that's just how it's going to be!" This kind of toxic leadership hurts people. And this version of vision casting relies too much on high control and fails to capture the diversity of ideas that are available in your team. Instead, a vision should be less rigid than the individual ideas you come up with. It shouldn't be a vision that only the church planter can see and use. It should be less like the individual blocks that make up the church and more like the container that these ideas fit inside of.

The job of the church planter—with input from their staff, leaders, and parent church—is to decide which slots get to be included in the vision. Then, as people come along, they will bring differently shaped blocks of their own—views, values, program ideas, and preferences. When they hand a leader a block, the leaders can turn to the sorting box in their hand to see if there's a slot that this idea might fit into.

For example, if someone says that they wish our church had a women's ministry, you can look at your imaginary sorting cube and ask yourself: *Does our church's vision have a spot for a women's ministry?* Go ahead. Grab the vision sorting cube and turn it in your hand. Where does it fit? Does it go into the star shape or the rectangle? They might want it to become a whole new ministry in the church, as if you're going to carve a new slot into the sorting cube itself. That's an option. You can always carve new holes in the sorting cube, but it's best to do that only when necessary. It's a lot of work to cut entirely new slots and if it doesn't work out, you will have slots there that you no longer use. Instead, try to fit them into an existing slot.

You could suggest to your member, after listening to their vision, that a new women's ministry would make sense as a small group. "It sounds like you're hoping to gather women together once a month for fellowship. A group like this is similar to other small groups we have. Let's start there and see where it goes." With their input, take their idea and find the hole in the sorting cube made for small groups.

It takes a little creativity to make this work. Sometimes an idea doesn't have an obvious slot. Imagine if someone wanted your church to support a local mission that meant a lot to them. Maybe it's a local homeless shelter that serves youth, or maybe it's an art studio for adults with disabilities, or any of a thousand worthy nonprofits. This happens often, and if you tried to put them all in our local mission's slot, the box would fill up quicker than you could imagine. In the end, your church would be stretched so thin, you wouldn't make any impact. So, when someone brings you a new local mission idea, there are a few slots that you can consider before making it a new ministry of the church. For example, one option would be to ask this person if they knew someone from that organization we could interview during worship. If so, it could easily fit into our church's Sunday morning slot and expand the diversity of voices you have in worship—that's a win-win! If this is the case, you can pass this idea on to the person scheduling your worship services to arrange a time for them to speak. Or it's possible that their suggestion might fit into a special offering—something you do one time and move on from. If not that, what if one of your small groups made it their focus and served at this nonprofit monthly? If they like that idea, then their suggestion can go in your small group slot.

This is deeply practical for organizational growth, because each slot has its own department and leadership. Starting a new ministry means a new department and a new leader, and this can create an overwhelmingly disorganized church. By taking ideas and working them into existing areas, you're able to use your vision and strategy to hold your congregation's passions in a way that empowers them without overpowering your capacity.

At times, you will have to say "*no*"—sometimes, because the box is full. Church plants have to say "*no*" more often than established churches because it's unhealthy for them to take on more than they can handle.

Sometimes you will have to say "*no*" because no matter how you look at it, it just doesn't fit. This could be an issue of justice, values, liability, capacity, or a hundred of other reasons. It's like they brought a moon to a sorting cube that doesn't have any moon slots! When this happens repeatedly, from the same person, it's likely the blocks they are holding don't belong to the sorting cube you've made. It's entirely possible they are looking for a different cube—an entirely different church. You can still love them and respect them, but also pray they find a church with slots that meet their needs.

Church plants will often attract very opinionated and strong-willed people who didn't fit into previous churches. If their visions line up with the church plant, great! If not, be careful and rest in the fact that your church isn't for everyone. In the end, this is just one way of bridging your church's vision with the ideas, passions, and perspectives of your church and launch team.

Next Steps

1. Write out all of your ideas for your new church plant.
2. After some time has passed, go back to your ideas and look for trends and big ideas.
3. Write out a summary of key words and phrases.
4. Use these to craft a mission and vision statement. Remember, a mission statement is what you hope to accomplish and who you hope to be. A vision statement is what your world, city, or neighborhood might look like if you are successful in your mission.
5. Use your vision and mission statement to write out a pitch.
6. Come up with 5-10 vision stories, or anecdotes that illustrate what you hope your church will look like.

7. Provide ways for friends, stakeholders, launch team members, and other leaders to speak into and contribute to the vision.

Church Planter's Toolkit

Go to churchplantershandbook.org to access the following resources related to this chapter:

- Choosing the Right Name for Your Church
- Forming a Mission & Vision Statement from Scratch
- "Tell Better Stories" eBook

Chapter 3

Ministry Action Plan

When I was a youth pastor, I took our kids on a mission trip to Vermont where we volunteered in a local park. It was a large hill in the middle of the community that they were turning into a place to hike and mountain bike. The local mission worked with the city to secure volunteers to help build this new place for the community. Two days in a row, we loaded up shovels and pickaxes and drove up the hill to build a new trail. The local volunteer piloting the process explained how trails were designed and built, and then he sent us out to remove large boulders and cut into the earth paths for the water to run off the paths, so they didn't erode.

Church planters can't help but consider how something came about—how it was created. The same was true for my experience in Vermont. It's where I realized the obvious: the trails we use in public parks are *designed*. Someone took time to lay out the trail, cut down the trees, remove the boulders, and build the bridges needed, so we could walk without ever having to think about how all those structures got there.

Have you ever tried hiking without a trail? Depending on where you are, you get lost easily. A trail makes enjoying nature easy. The difference between hiking a well-established trail and building one is the difference between working in an established church and starting one. When hiking an established trail, you can flip into autopilot until you reach your destination and enjoy the view. When building a trail, there's no autopilot and if you haven't surveyed the land, studied the map, or paid attention to your compass, bearings, and terrain, you'll get lost.

Building trails—being a literal trailblazer—requires planning and strategy, surveying the entire land, finding the best route to the destination, removing obstacles, and building necessary structures to make it safe for visitors who might come later. This is the difference between trail blazing and trail building. A trailblazer will push through uncharted territory, but only those following close behind are going to benefit from their path. Trailblazers aren't concerned with those coming after them. They are there for the sake of the adventure. On the other hand, trail-builders are much more careful and thorough. They think through the best path for all visitors, placing the right signs, installing bridges and steps, and making the entire experience as enjoyable as possible for those coming after them. They aren't there for the adventure. They are there to build something others can enjoy for generations to come.

This is the job of the church planter. You're not just a trailblazer, you're a trail builder.

When building a Ministry Action Plan (MAP) for your new church it's a lot like building a trail:

1. Know where you're headed.
2. Survey the land.
3. Lay out your path.
4. Remove the obstacles and hazards.
5. Build the structures to make it easier for people to follow.

When you have these, you're ready to open the trail for visitors. This is how you launch a church from scratch. Laying out each of these into a plan, with action items and timeline becomes your MAP that will lead you to your destination and that's what you will learn to build in this chapter.

1. Know Where You're Headed

Start with the end in mind. Are you building a trail that leads to a waterfall or a mountain top? Or does it just meander through the woods, perfect for a peaceful stroll? The trail you build depends entirely on where you want to go, just like the plan you use for your church plant will be based entirely on the kind of church you hope to build. This is why you need to spend adequate time clarifying your mission and vision, so that your plan is taking you where you want to go. What picture have you painted for your launch team that gets them excited to go on a journey? Starting a church is hard, and knowing where it's headed will give your team the motivation they need. Few people will hike miles, uphill, without knowing first if there's a beautiful view or waterfall at the end of the journey. If the goal is to have a trail that meanders, and it's more about the people you go on the journey with, great! But make that clear. If someone wants to see a waterfall, and they end up on a peaceful stroll that only loops around, they will be disappointed.

Know where you're headed.

2. Survey the Land

It is always unwise to lay out a trail without first becoming familiar with the topography, density of trees, landscape, canyons, and rivers. The routes you could come up with without the topography in mind, might be straight, but you're likely to get stuck and stranded. A straight line does nothing to take into account the crevices, cliffs, boulders, trees, and valleys along the way.

Before creating a strategy, you must know what you're working with.

Here are some ideas you can use to survey the land for your church planting journey.

Set the boundaries. Will you be working within a neighborhood, city, village, or county? Set the boundaries of your church's area, knowing that this doesn't have to be strict. For example, many churches in the city gather people from all over the city, and so when thinking through their target area, sometimes they might consider a neighborhood and other times they might think about the entire city.

There's a church located in a small town in Ohio that used these principles for setting their boundaries. When working on their mission and vision, they would at times talk about their town, but at other times, talk about ministry in the wider county. Churches often have multiple areas they are trying to serve. This is what it means when John Wesley said, "the world is my parish." Jesus said something similar when he sent his disciples out to be the church, telling them "You will be my witnesses in Jerusalem, in all Judea and Samaria, and to the ends of the earth" (Acts 1:8). What is your Jerusalem, Judaea, and Samaria? Setting these boundaries will help you narrow your focus and understand the topography of your route.

Run a Demographic Study on the Area. Once you've set your boundaries, run a demographic study on your designated area. Like a topographic map of a park, demographic studies show you the cultural landscape of your area. MissionInsite is a great resource, as it provides detailed information for customized areas, including simple demographics like population, age, average income, etc., but also unique insights like average media consumption, religious views, and more. Whether you go with them or another company, having a detailed demographic study on the area you're planting is essential to developing your strategy.

In a recent demographic study for a small rural area, the pastor learned that there was a perception that churches "only want people's money." This was important to be aware of because this church was in the middle of a fundraising campaign. During an event where the pastor was sharing their vision for this fundraising campaign, a few members of the church started brainstorming fundraising ideas they had, like bake sales and other community-based events. Thankfully, equipped with this statistical data, they were able to pivot, avoiding any fundraising events that would ask the wider community to support. Instead, they decided to focus on those in the church—those committed to the mission already. The campaign was all about raising money for the church to do more outreach and reach new people. If they started this fundraising by asking people outside the church to give, the church might have hurt their end goal by only playing into the cultural assumptions prevalent in their designated area. This is why it's important to survey the land. You must know what you're working with. When looking at a demographic study, here are a few of the things to consider:

Religious Views: Do people like church? Do they think positively about it? Do most people identify as a person of faith already?

In most areas of the country, the majority of people who went to church but stopped attending. If that's the case in your area, your job isn't to tell them about Jesus for the first time. They knew plenty about Jesus. Your job is to present a different way of doing church, addressing the stories and pain that had pushed them away. A few years ago, Barna put out a book called "You Lost Me."[1] In the book, they laid out various reasons people have left church. They grouped their findings into these categories:

- **Overprotective**: A growing number of people leave the church because it's unwilling to try new things, think differently, or take risks.
- **Shallow**: Young people see the shallow relationships in many congregations as a barrier to honest community. They are able to develop more authentic and vulnerable relationships outside the church.
- **Anti-science**: Science asks questions and tests new ideas. The church appears anti-science.
- **Repressive**: When it comes to issues of human sexuality and gender expression, many churches are repressive instead of liberating.
- **Exclusive**: Is there room in our faith for us to have honest relationships with people who don't agree with us? Some feel the church is too exclusive and isolating.
- **Doubtless**: Churches that people left discourage asking questions or doubting the teaching of the church.

Other reasons people might leave the church include abuse, toxic theology, authoritarian cultures, and more. Applying this study to your demographic area, you can take these reasons, flip them around, and make them into commitments for visitors.

Our Commitment to You:

- You'll never be judged, no matter who you are, or what you believe.
- You can share the real you, as much or as little as you want.
- Your views on science or politics don't have to be checked at the door.

- You will never be expected to hide your doubts or questions.
- You won't be forced to do something you disagree with.

Know the religious views of the population you're hoping to serve and build your MAP accordingly. It's not about changing who you are to reach people. It's about knowing the barriers and challenges that are in front of you so you can build the bridges needed to overcome them.

Age & Season of Life: If you run a demographic report on your area and the majority of the people who live there are empty nesters with grown up children who moved away, it's probably not wise to launch your church built around children's ministry.

Income: If you're planting in a wealthy area, it will be much easier to become self-sustaining quickly. If you're planting in a less-resourced area, you might need grants and outside funders to become self-sustaining. Wealth is not equally distributed in America, and neighborhoods in large cities are often deeply segregated due to generations of redlining. The church planter can overcome this barrier by building a mixed-income community that represents diverse neighborhoods. Otherwise, a church in a wealthy neighborhood will fail to meet the call of Jesus, and a church in an under-resourced neighborhood will fail to meet the needs of its members. This should directly impact your MAP, which should lay out your plans for fundraising and long-term sustainability.

Political Identities: If you're moving into a conservative neighborhood and your church is going to be progressive, be ready to deal with the conflict and tension that comes from that. Know that you might not reach as many people as a conservative church, and your strategy should take this into account, giving yourself a longer launch season to become sustainable.

There are countless other categories you should consider when you get your demographic report back. Read through it like a trail builder would study the topography of a land. Where are the valleys? What rivers need to be traversed? What natural trails exist already that we can take advantage of?

3. Lay out Your Path

With the map on the table, and the land properly surveyed, you're ready to take a marker and sketch out the path you hope to take. In church planting, this includes your plans and strategy for worship, community engagement, local mission, discipleship, children's ministry, etc. You might host launch events and/or develop a strategy to reach new people. Eventually you will need administrative processes, an organizational chart, and a church budget.

How will you fund the ministry? What leaders will you need to accomplish the work? What will their job descriptions be?

Laying out your plan will take a lot of your time. It will involve solving dozens of problems, implementing creative solutions, and spending hundreds of hours developing administrative processes. To help, let's think through these as a route—or timeline. For many church plants, the strategy can be divided into the following phases:

Phase 1: Discernment & Laying the Groundwork

This includes training, reading books, time in prayer, reflecting on your calling, and crafting an initial mission and vision. It might also include finding a parent church or some kind of commissioning, sending organization, or denominational appointment.

Phase 2: The Launch Season

This includes meeting new people, developing financial processes, building teams, planning outreach events, marketing and branding, and guest readiness. All of this leads to a launch of your church. It can launch large, with a big worship service, or launch gradually, slowly over time. Different models have different benefits.

Phase 3: Post-Launch

Now that your church is off to a good start, it's time to consider signature local ministries, discipleship, visitor follow-up events, board formation, and any other process or program needed to accomplish your ministry. This book focuses on the first two phases. For your MAP, you should lay out the plans for all three. With the right plan, you can begin building your church.

4. Remove the Obstacles

When we volunteered to help build a trail in Vermont, we spent hours removing stones and boulders. The path was meant to be for both walking and mountain biking, and the large stones and boulders made it dangerous. The problem with removing boulders, is that you don't realize how big the stone is until you start digging around it. Sometimes the part that's sticking out is just the tip of the iceberg. The same is true for church planting. The obstacles you face should be obvious, but the solution might be more complicated than you originally thought. What might seem like a distant problem could turn into something major the closer you get to it and the longer you dig around it.

Every church plant is different, and each will have its unique challenges. For many, finding a location is a major challenge. If you already have a space, then that's one thing you don't have to worry about. Be grateful—but if you're obligated to use a space, you might have a different set of problems, like accessibility, limited freedom to update or decorate, or that old church smell that new people notice when they walk in. Whether you have a space or not, there are always problems to address. For some, it might be a lack of clarity around their mission or vision. For others, it might feel impossible to find the right staff person, whether it be music, children's ministry, or administration. Finding a good worship leader and children's leader remains one of the biggest struggles in launching a new church centered on Sunday morning.

Whatever it is, take time looking at your plan and name the biggest obstacles that might keep you from accomplishing your goal. Where are you headed? What would keep you from getting there? How will you remove these obstacles?

5. Build Structures to Connect It All Together

Hocking Hills State Park is located in Southeast Ohio, with beautiful hikes that wind through a small canyon, with stairs to help you get down and back up, and bridges that crisscross the creek. If you have a chance to go, you'll run into a few bridges. One in particular is beautiful, in brutal industrial style, made entirely out of disconnected cement pillars and platforms. Can you imagine what it took to make such a bridge? How did they get so much concrete into the canyon? Did they have a helicopter drop it off? Was it carted in by foot? Is there a road nearby that is hidden from the trail? Building a bridge at the bottom of a canyon, without any road access, has real challenges, but the great thing is that if it's a reliable bridge, it only has to be built once. After that, hundreds of people can easily cross without ever thinking about the work it took to build it. Without these structures, there's no trail. People will get stuck at the bottom of a canyon on one side of the river or the other.

There are certain things that happen in church planting that are hard work and will require great faith and energy, but the hope is that if you're building it right, it will last, and hundreds will be able to enjoy it without ever having to think about how it came to be. Here are some of the hardest things you'll do as a church planter that visitors don't have to think about:

1. Figuring out your church name, logo, mission and vision, branding, values…
2. Finding a location
3. Building a worship team
4. Building a children's ministry
5. Developing guest follow-up processes
6. Forming a leadership team
7. Writing church policy
8. Building a compelling website
9. Recruit staff
10. Build a unique culture
11. Develop discipleship process
12. Launch new ministries in the community

The list could go on and on and on, but like a bridge built along a hike, the hope is you learn to do it right, and when it's done, it can be used and enjoyed without anyone worrying how it got there. Visitors will experience these as if they have always been there. They don't know, and they don't need to know, the blood, sweat, and tears that will go into making each of these a reality.

Consider your plan so far. What structures do you need to build to ensure people are able to come along with you in this journey?

> Growing Generous Givers
>
> Your ministry action plan needs to include your plans for becoming self-sustaining. This means your projected income will match your projected expenses. If you plan to launch a house church of 30 people but also want to be paid full-time, with health benefits, you will need to explain where you expect to get those additional funds. If you're launching in a community that can't afford a full-time pastor, you will need to have plans for outside funding. Donors give to projects that are well-thought out and have a clear plan. You will do much better at raising support if you are able to explain how you're going to reach your goals. In this way, a ministry action plan is also a fundraising tool.

Church Planter's Toolkit

Go to churchplantershandbook.org to access the following resources related to this chapter:

- **Custom Church Timeline:** All it takes is 5 minutes and 16 questions, and you will receive hundreds of ideas to get started laying out your next steps in a 10-month custom timeline.
- **Ministry Action Plan (MAP) Worksheet:** This worksheet is a structured tool designed to help church planters and ministry

leaders clarify their vision, mission, and strategy for launching a new church or ministry.

- **Worship Attendance Calculator:** This calculator helps you estimate your launch team growth, and first worship service attendance based on key factors like outreach efforts and team engagement.

Chapter 4

Parent Churches, Denominations, and Challenging the Status Quo

Jesus launched his new vision for the world in a deeply saturated religious community with high controls and expectations of all participants. He offered something new and fresh, but those who were deeply committed to the "way things were" found his teachings not only problematic but heretical. In the end, they killed him to squash his radical ideas.

Tension happens when something new or "radical" pushes against deep-rooted traditions. Instead of embracing diversity and innovation, unhealthy leaders can be threatened by new ideas, fearing their loss of power or influence. When this happens, diversity of thought and expression can be seen as "impure" or "dangerous." Rob Bell, once hailed as a leading voice in American evangelicalism, particularly through his Mars Hill Bible Church and popular *NOOMA* video series, experienced a dramatic fall from grace within the evangelical community. His shift began with his 2011 book *Love Wins*, in which he questioned traditional views of hell and eternal damnation, embracing a more inclusive, universalist perspective on salvation. This departure from evangelical orthodoxy provoked a strong backlash from evangelical leaders. As a result, Bell found himself increasingly ostracized from mainstream evangelical circles, eventually stepping away from his pastoral role and embracing a more progressive, spiritual path that resonated beyond traditional evangelicalism. He now writes science fiction and paints.

The church isn't always a safe place for new or divergent ideas. The theology of hell is a good example of some of the darker themes that arise when we challenge the status quo. Rob Bell wasn't just challenging a particular doctrine; he was putting at risk one of the tools used by evangelicals to motivate their congregations to action and keep their disciples committed to evangelism. By challenging evangelical theology on hell, he was putting at risk the authority, power, and influence evangelical church leaders have over their communities.

Jesus offered similar challenges to long-held beliefs, specifically fasting and the Sabbath. These practices were another example of how religious leaders wielded power and influence over people's daily behaviors. When you consider the significance of fasting and the Sabbath, it's obvious why they were so important to religious rules. There is nothing more basic than people's relationship to food and how they spend their time. Even though the ruler's teachings on the Sabbath and fasting were biblical and socially acceptable ways to show religious devotion, Jesus didn't make his disciples do either.

> They said to him, "John's disciples often fast and pray, and so do the disciples of the Pharisees, but yours go on eating and drinking." (Luke 5:33)

Jesus responded to this challenge with two parables that involve the flexibility of fabrics.

> He told them this parable: "No one tears a piece out of a new garment to patch an old one. Otherwise, they will have torn the new garment, and the patch from the new will not match the old.
>
> "And no one pours new wine into old wineskins. Otherwise, the new wine will burst the skins; the wine will run out and the wineskins will be ruined. No, new wine must be poured into new wineskins. And no one after drinking old wine wants the new, for they say, 'The old is better.'" (Luke 5:36-39)

Both parables deal with the rigidity or flexibility of fabric, whether that be the garment you wear or the use of leather to make a pouch to hold wine.

Old garments, exposed to the sun and heat of the Mediterranean climate would become brittle. New fabrics were flexible, but also over time would shrink just as the old had. Given this, new fabric wouldn't work for repairing an old garment, for it would shrink and tear the garment more. The same issue of rigidity is applied to wineskins. They couldn't hold new wine for the wine would ferment and expand, tearing the fragile and rigid old wineskin.

Jesus allowed his disciples to relax on the Sabbath and eat as they pleased, abandoning the rigidity of the religious establishment, because the vision Jesus had for life couldn't be contained by such inflexible containers. In the end, Jesus was bringing a kingdom for the poor, hurting, blind, and sick. His disciples needed to focus on this mission and not get distracted by the staunch rules of Sabbath-keeping or worrying about who they shared a meal with. Worrying about these things was not only a distraction but a barrier to accomplishing the mission. How could they open a table for all those who have been set aside or overlooked by the religious establishment if they were fasting or worried about who was sitting at their table? (Matthew 9:10-17, Mark 2:15-22, Luke 5:29-39)

Old Wine Isn't Bad; New Wine Isn't Better

These two parables end with a curious line: "And no one after drinking old wine wants the new, for they say, 'The old is better.'"

Jesus, the one who is ushering in a new expression of faith, points out that people tend to prefer the old. Some wines can improve with age, but it's not always the case. Some get worse with age, due to many different reasons. Jesus isn't necessarily talking about the quality of the wine, but the personal preferences of religious leaders. People tend to prefer what they are used to. Those in church prefer church the way it is—of course they do! That's why they are in church to begin with. Jesus didn't come only to reach those already living a good Jewish life. He came for the hurt and marginalized, too.

When we do something new, those who prefer things "the way they were" will share their opinions loud and clear.

"The old is better!"

This comes up in a lot of different ways, like when a room of clergy rail on contemporary music or complain about how some pastors don't wear robes. Or when a room of evangelical pastors look down on churches that don't have Grammy-award winning worship leaders or original worship albums. Or when a mega-church pastor tells his associate pastors to buy better clothes or when the worship leader puts together a Pinterest account of appropriate clothing for those singing in the band, so they live up to the church's brand on stage.

All of these are sadly real examples of people pushing their preferences and long-held traditions. When you feel the pressure to conform to a majority expression, whether that be pressure to have a church with organ music and robes, or a church with a light show and trendy jeans, remind yourself: Church planters don't start new churches to have more of the same. Church planters start a new church to make sure there's *new* wine for those who haven't gotten any—those who have been overlooked. The church needs to start new churches so we can have enough wine for everyone (John 2:1-12) especially after we invite people who haven't been invited before (Luke 14:12-24).

Sometimes new wine takes time to ferment, that's why some old wine is better. Established churches will outshine and outperform new church starts in many ways. Established congregations have had time to develop processes, culture, financial health, and more. They might have the people and members to offer dozens of programs and make a huge impact. A new church start, on the other hand, might struggle in its first year to have enough volunteers to hold weekly services, let alone a full-fledged youth ministry. Church plants must prioritize and not take on more than they are able, or they won't last.

It's unfair to compare church plants and established churches. In fact, we need to remember the sobering truth that a church plant will become established, God willing, and future spiritual entrepreneurs and generations will find your "new" church too rigid and stuck in its ways. These new generations will go out and start new churches or help established churches reinvent themselves, just like this generation is doing—just like previous generations had done before them.

Never forget that every church that has ever existed was a church plant at some point. Churches are not good or bad because they are old or new. They are simply located on different points along the same life cycle. One might pursue new ideas while the other is strong enough to hold high quality wine, but we need both. The simple truth not mentioned in this passage is that new wine and old wine are often stored in the same cellar, which means at the very least, we need to get along.

The Parent/Child Matrix

Not everyone has had positive experiences growing up. Many friends and parishioners have had parents who were abusive, manipulative, distant, unavailable, selfish, childish, and everything in between. Many choose to cut ties with their parents entirely because of the overbearing toxicity.

Even when a relationship is positive, it isn't always easy. As I grew up, my perspective on faith and politics changed. I began to question core beliefs my parents held, creating tension in our relationship. I moved away and learned and experienced things my parents never had the chance to experience, and my faith changed as a result. The greater it changed, the greater the tension arose between me and my parents. Thankfully, my parents are emotionally healthy and committed to loving their kids, so while we disagree on politics and theology, I know they love me, and we remain close.

In the same way my relationship with my parents became tense when disagreements on politics enter the conversation, there can be significant tension between parent churches and church plants on differences in policies, theology, or expression. A parent/child relationship is a helpful lens when thinking about the relationship to launching something new within the framework of accepted norms.

As cultural differences between generations increase exponentially, we need to lean into hard conversations that seek mutual understanding. This is especially true with the advancement of technology and the rapid changes happening between generations. The **Parent/Child Matrix** below can help do this. There are four, intersecting categories in parent/child relationships when thinking about church planting. There are parent churches that have a healthy and unhealthy relationship with the church plant, and parent churches that are similar or different than the church plant.

	Healthy	Unhealthy
Similar		
Different		

"Healthy" and "unhealthy" refers to the health/unhealth of the parent church (or denomination) in its relationship to the church plant. When thinking about the health of a parent church, consider specifically the emotional or spiritual maturity of the church/denomination and its leaders in the following categories:

> **Self-awareness**: Understanding your own needs, values, and emotional triggers is foundational to healthy leadership. Those in leadership need to understand their weaknesses and strengths, what makes them unique, and the limitations of their reach and effectiveness. Without self-awareness, tensions can rise between the parent church and anything that appears to challenge its already-established worldview.
>
> **Clear communication**: Expressing the needs, limits, and boundaries openly and assertively is vital in any leadership relationship, whether it be between the senior pastor and the church planter,

director of new church starts and the planter, or a church board and the pastor. Healthy boundaries are maintained through respectful, clear conversations where both parties understand each other's expectations. It's been said often but remains important in healthy relationships: *clear is kind.* Withholding information, lack of transparency, talking behind people's backs, or offering misinformation is a sign of an unhealthy organization and will cause problems in the church planting process.

Mutual respect: A healthy parent church or sending organization will practice mutual respect, especially with theology or ideas that counter its core values. All levels of church leadership need to honor and value each other's boundaries, feelings, and perspectives. Ensuring that our boundaries don't infringe on others' rights while advocating for our own is a delicate balance but essential to emotionally healthy leadership.

Curiosity: The world is filled with great diversity and differences in thought and opinion, and there is no lack of diversity in theology and expressions of faith. A healthy church and healthy church leaders should respond to new ideas and different opinions with good questions, rooted in sincere curiosity, that help those they are mentoring process, adjust, and implement the ideas they are considering.

Conflict resolution: Conflict is unavoidable. Humans are fragile. People have baggage, triggers, fears, and insecurities. Misunderstandings happen. The question isn't whether there is conflict between a church plant and its parent church or sending organization, the question is *how* it will be handled when it happens. Are complaints or concerns brushed under the rug, ignored, or dismissed? Or are people heard and their concerns validated? Are those in top leadership able to apologize for mistakes, or does the church/organization have a posture that doesn't allow for such humility? Does the church have a track record for conflict resolution that includes the voices of all those impacted, giving everyone the benefit of the doubt? Or does the organization tend to avoid or dismiss conflict or make assumptions about those involved?

Consistency: Finally, a healthy church and its leadership will be consistent. Upholding our boundaries and expectations consistently, rather than bending them out of guilt, pressure, or privilege, helps maintain emotional health and integrity. Inconsistent boundaries can lead to confusion and resentment, both for yourself and others in leadership. When leaders make up the rules as they go along, or make exceptions to some while not for others, confusion and hurt can mark the entire church planting journey.

When considering the health of a parent church, there are a lot of other factors beyond these, but none of those factors are greater than emotional and spiritual health. For example, a church planter might look for a parent church or sending organization with lots of resources and a large budget. In fact, it might be your default to think of a parent church as "healthy" if it has money in the budget and large attendance numbers, but a small emotionally healthy church offering what little support they can is 100 times better than a large church or organization that is toxic.

Consider where you and your parent church (or equivalent) scores along the healthy to unhealthy spectrum. Is it healthy, unhealthy, or somewhere in the middle?

Similar/Different

Next, let's look at the vertical axis. "Similar" and "different" refers to the culture and practices of a church plant compared to its parent church (or equivalent). Here are a few topics to consider when trying to measure this:

1. **Finances & Stewardship**: How do the financial practices align? Does the parent church rely on traditional methods like physical offerings, while the church plant uses online giving? Is the parent church generous or focused on scarcity?
2. **Worship Style & Leadership**: Compare worship styles—traditional versus contemporary—and other elements like children's programs or the use of vestments. Additionally, how does the role of the pastor differ? Will your focus be on outreach and community, while the parent church prioritizes pastoral care?

3. **Generational & Cultural Dynamics**: Will the church plant attract a younger, more diverse congregation? Are there significant differences in generational values or racial/ethnic makeup that could impact how both churches connect and communicate?
4. **Location & Demographics**: Is the church plant in a different setting compared to the parent church—urban, suburban, or rural?
5. **Governance & Decision-Making**: How are decisions made in each church? Does the parent church rely on committees, while the church plant will operate with a more staff-driven approach? Consider how differing governance styles may affect leadership interactions.
6. **Volunteer Engagement & Leadership**: In a church plant, leadership roles are often filled quickly due to the immediate need. In the parent church, are new people given room to lead without hoops to jump through? How do volunteer motivations differ? Are volunteers mission-driven in the church plant versus serving out of an unhealthy obligation in the parent church?
7. **Discipleship & Theology**: Are there different approaches to discipleship? For example, the church plant may focus on small groups, while the parent church uses traditional Sunday school. Also, assess theological alignment—particularly on contentious issues like LGBTQ+ inclusion, racism, DEI, or social activism. Are these issues discussed or avoided?
8. **Innovation & Flexibility**: How open is the parent church to new ideas? Is it slower to adapt, while a church plant often has to thrive on rapid innovation?
9. **Hope & Vision for the Future**: A church plant's vitality often comes from a hopeful vision for the future. Does the parent church share this sense of optimism and growth, or does it face a more uncertain path?

In the end, you're trying to decide whether your new endeavor is going to reflect what those in your community are used to or are you going to offer something that might confuse them.

With that in mind, we end up with four parent/child relationships: Mentor, Advocate, Mirror, and Antagonist.

	Healthy	Unhealthy
Similar	*Mentor*	*Mirror*
Different	*Advocate*	*Antagonist*

Understanding where your supporting body falls within these categories can help you navigate the relationship with clarity. There are four primary types of relationships a church planter might experience with its parent church, network, or denomination. We will start with the hardest and work towards the easiest. In each of these, we will use Jesus's relationship with the religious establishment as a backdrop for theological reflection.

1. Antagonist

The Gospels tell story after story of Jesus facing the antagonism of the religious establishment. The Pharisees, Sadducees, and crowds in Jerusalem, found his teachings to be disruptive and dangerous.

The same can be true today, anytime there's an authority relationship that is *unhealthy,* and the church plant is doing something *different.*

This happens often, like when a majority white church hires a church planter of a different ethnicity, who quits less than a year into the process. Or when an aging congregation gets paired with a church planter, but the failure to understand the vision causes more pain than help. Or when an established church hires someone to reach new people and then fires them when they do things that would reach new people.

When a church plant pastor is paired with an *unhealthy* congregation that doesn't share its vision, the parent church will nine times out of ten become the antagonist, holding back the church planter from reaching new people and causing additional stress and discouragement. The same can be said when a church plant is launching out of an unhealthy conference, association, or network. When an organization doesn't have healthy practices, like self-awareness, mutual respect, and clear communication, it's unbelievably difficult to feel supported when pursuing something different or new.

This can be seen in the smallest of issues, like online giving. Some aging traditional churches can be weary of online giving—even in a post-pandemic world, this still happens—but a church plant must rely heavily on online giving, like most churches today. When you come from a parent church that also embraces online giving, you will never once have to explain online giving to your leaders. Whereas in some churches, something like online giving might require ten different conversations. In a similar church, assumed practices like this won't even require a conversation. It will be assumed, and with all to do, one less conversation makes a difference. You might think that having these conversations isn't a big deal, but in reality, these kinds of conversations, especially when leaders are emotionally unhealthy, add up and can do a lot to drain a church plant's limited momentum.

A new church must spend money on things that don't exist yet. For example, a new church that wants to reach children, needs to hire a children's person for the kids they want to reach—not the kids they currently have. This kind of financial investment can be difficult if a parent church hasn't had children's ministry in years, and when it did, it was 100% volunteer led.

If you're planting out of a church or denomination that prefers not to invest money into vital ministries, be sure to set healthy boundaries. Does the parent church get the final say on how funds at the new church start are spent? Can the new church start only spend money on things the parent church agrees to? Will there be countless hoops to jump through before money can be spent?

These questions can make us uncomfortable, but they are far less uncomfortable than investing three years into a church plant, only to be told "no" every step of the way and then feel blamed when it fails to take off. This has happened time and time again. Church planting is hard, even if everything works in your favor. When those who are supposed to support you make it more difficult, church planting can do immense damage to the mind and heart of the leaders.

The real issue isn't with a parent church saying "no" to requests. The real issue is all the doubts and questions and discouragement and hoops that you have to jump through along the way. It's not that questions are bad, it's that questions—especially judgmental questions—take time and energy to address, and the energy spent on questions could have been spent meeting new people instead of fueling the self-doubt of the church planter. Ask anyone serving in a cross-cultural setting and they will likely agree with this: operating in a space where there isn't a shared, mutual understanding requires loads of additional energy and effort to move things forward.

My advice to church planters: When your parent church or sending organization is an antagonist to your vision, and you're struggling to live out of your call in an emotionally healthy way, the best you can do is distance yourself from them. If you can find a different parent church or organization, it might make it a lot easier for you. If you can't, try and distance yourself to a degree that won't cause additional problems. Then, do your best to provide updates and information that come as close to satisfying their expectations as you can without distracting yourself from what God has called you to do. In the end, try not to stir up conflict by being professional and clear. You can't control what your parent church or authority figures do, but you can control how you respond.

2. Mirror

While the majority of the time the religious rulers pushed against Jesus, challenging him and questioning, there are a few examples of Jesus pushing back. In Matthew 23, Jesus offers a series of scathing criticism against the Pharisees and Sadducees. In verse 15, he adds this to the list of remarks:

> Woe to you, teachers of the law and Pharisees, you hypocrites! You travel over land and sea to win a single convert, and when you have succeeded, you make them twice as much a child of hell as you are. (Matthew 23:15)

Jesus is describing toxic discipleship, where emotionally and spiritually unhealthy leaders raise up new unhealthy leaders.

If your church or your church's leadership practices are all you've ever known, it's hard to imagine doing anything different. All you can do is *mirror* what you've seen whether it causes harm or not.

Unhealthy leaders produce more unhealthy leaders. Hurt people will hurt people (who go on to hurt people who hurt more people). With mirrors, there is no creativity, growth, or authenticity. These is only the shallow duplications of unhealthy theology. Toxicity is a cycle until someone steps in and stops it.

Today, hundreds of churches are launched every year that refuse to let women lead, discriminate against LGBTQ+ people, push people towards Christian nationalism, and tell people they are going to hell if they don't fall in line.

Jesus makes it clear that not all discipleship is good.

When an unhealthy church produces more churches, the world ends up with more unhealthy churches—even when the church planter has a different vision.

At times, church planters can become aware of a parent church or denomination's unhealthy practices but feel ill-equipped to challenge or go against the status quo but struggle to stand up against the systems and authorities that dictate their ministry. For example, pastors who affirm LGBTQ+ people might not share this publicly with their congregation or denomination because they know they could lose their jobs or limit their opportunities if they did.

When church leaders feel the church should be different but have a desire to appease those in power and fall in line, all they are really doing is mirroring the behavior of the parent church even if they don't personally endorse it.

It can be something more benign than a deep theological issue, like a church planter wants to use contemporary worship songs but knows the parent church would never support it, so they launch with traditional music anyways. Or a church plant that knows great children's ministry is important to reaching their neighborhood, but they can't launch with children's ministry because their aging parent church is threatened by it. What if a church or denomination decides the King James Version is the only version of scripture to use, and even though the church planter doesn't agree, they go along anyway. There are dozens of examples like this throughout church history and you can think of a few yourself. When a church planter perpetuates unhealthy practices or feels pressured to fall in line, it's unhealthy for both the church plant and the parent church.

If you find yourself mirroring unhealthy behaviors or values, you can either try to remove yourself or actively go against the accepted norm. If you engage in this kind of creative protest, be prepared to face additional troubles. If your goal is to change the system, be strategic and keep going. I'm grateful our LGBTQ+ clergy in the United Methodist Church stayed even when the denomination pushed back.

If advocating for change is not a part of your calling, I pray that you can find a community that will allow you to embrace a new vision for church.

3. Advocate

If you're planting a church that is *different* from your parent church, but your parent church is emotionally *healthy*, you should have a good advocate who can protect you and defend you in the face of those who are confused or threatened by your ideas.

While Jesus and the religious rulers of his day had very real tensions, not all interactions were negative. Two examples are of well-respected religious leaders who supported the status quo but defended and advocated for Jesus, even though they didn't seem to fully understand what Jesus was trying to do.

One example is from John 4, where Nicodemus visits Jesus. They have a profound conversation that seems to go over Nicodemus's head. He can't understand Jesus's teachings on being born again and how the Spirit of God is like the wind going where it pleases. His old wineskin brain can't process these new ideas quick enough! Still, much later in the gospel of John, Nicodemus re-emerges in the story, standing up for Jesus. When the rulers are looking for a way to bring an end to Jesus's teaching, Nicodemus says:

> Does our law condemn a man without first hearing him to find out what he has been doing? (John 7:51)

Nicodemus, a leader in the status quo, uses his influence to give Jesus the benefit of the doubt.

A similar story comes later in the book of Acts. Just like with Jesus, the religious leaders are looking to bring an end to the disciples and their radical teachings, but before they could, another respected religious ruler speaks up:

> When they heard this, they were furious and wanted to put them to death. But a Pharisee named Gamaliel, a teacher of the law, who was honored by all the people, stood up in the Sanhedrin and ordered that the men be put outside for a little while. (Acts 5:33-34)

With the disciples out of the room, no longer being berated, he gives a beautiful speech, that ends with this simple decree:

> I advise you: Leave these men alone! Let them go! For if their purpose or activity is of human origin, it will fail. But if it is from God, you will not be able to stop these men; you will only find yourselves fighting against God. (Acts 5:38-39)

This is what an advocate does. They can speak up to the masses who would challenge the "crazy" ideas and "heretical" thoughts of new generations, suggesting everyone calm down and give them a chance.

Anytime a church plant is doing something that the parent church or denomination struggles to understand, their only hope is that someone with respect and credibility stands up for them.

It's far easier to launch a *similar* church out of a *healthy* congregation, but just because that is the easiest doesn't mean it's always the best. We need new churches that are diverse, creative, and provide alternatives to the majority church experience, which means we need more advocates. If we only ever plant churches that resemble established churches, we will only ever reach people who would likely attend that kind of church. In the end, learning to support and understand faith experiences that are different from our own is far more beneficial than striving to keep things the same.

When a parent church invests in a church that is intentionally different from itself, it's important to recognize its own limitations. A healthy church will do this because it's self-aware. This is true if the church plant is launching out of a suburban church and planting in an urban environment, a white church launching a church led by people of color, or a boomer church launching a Gen Z church. In each of these examples, the parent church or sending organization might not have the best advice for a church plant, but a healthy parent church won't take that personally.

Imagine if Gamaliel or Nicodemus took it upon themselves to mentor Jesus or his disciples?

How would that go?

It'd be like King Saul trying to get David to wear his prized armor.

It'd be like putting new wine into old wineskins.

It wouldn't work.

Advocates aren't mentors. They need to cheer the planter on, ensuring the church planter has resources they need that match the culture and vision they are trying to launch. A non-affirming evangelical mega-church isn't the ideal parent church for an affirming, inclusive church plant, but if they are emotionally and spiritually healthy, they will be able to remain friendly and provide appropriate support. This isn't to say that every parent has to fully endorse and financially support every church plant. It simply means that healthy boundaries and clear communication will keep the relationship civil and respectful, minimizing future harm.

If your parent church falls into the advocate quadrant, provide them with clear and meaningful ways for them to support you. But don't expect to get great input on how to do it, because you're doing something they haven't done before. Instead, seek advice and input from coaches that more closely resemble your vision and target population.

4. Mentor

If your parent church is generally healthy and you're planting a church that is similar, then you are in luck! You have a great mentor in planting a new church. If this is you, lean into the advice, perspective, and input from your parent church and their leaders. Be grateful you have their input!

Our Experience

I got to know Paul Risler, pastor at Central Avenue UMC, chatting mostly online. At one point I messaged him about church planting. He was, at the time, looking for a new associate. He wasn't interested in planting a church and I wasn't interested in being an associate, but in church planting you not only have to put yourself out there, but you also have to help people see how apparent competing ideas can co-exist. This takes initiative, creativity, and out-of-box thinking.

I asked him if he would be open to someone being an associate for a season, to learn the way of life at that church, and then be sent out to plant a similar church.

I messaged Paul, asking, "How many people are there living in Columbus, Cincinnati, or Dayton that once attended Central and would get excited and supportive if Central planted a church there?"

Remember: *you have not, because you ask not.*

I went on to try and convince him, and in classic Paul fashion, he was encouraging but said this. "Let's talk about this in a couple of weeks. Right now, I have too much on my plate to give it serious brain power... But I'll pray and start thinking. A network of Central church plants. Hummm…"

The seed had been planted.

I ended the conversation with one last pitch, playing off the idea of a church in Columbus, Ohio, a city centrally located in our state: "I want the first church plant to be called Central City Church."

I sent that on August 28, 2013.

Four years later my wife and I moved to Columbus and launched Central City Church.

Our church launched a congregation that was similar to our parent church in many ways, and in the ways we are different, our parent church has always leaned into authenticity and healthy boundaries, supporting us from a distance even when they don't agree with us—much like any good parents.

In fact, as grateful as I am for my parents and their respect and support for me even in our differences, I'm grateful for our parent church. They have been generous, compassionate, supportive, and available to help in any way they could. When you find a healthy church, there is much you can gain from it. Here is what we learned and gained from our parent church.

Financial Support

Our parent church provided the funding we needed to get the church off to a healthy financial start. Not only can you receive funding, but when you launch out of a church that reflects your vision for generosity, you are able to duplicate their financial processes, fundraising strategies, donor management, and more.

> Growing Generous Givers
>
> Maintaining a healthy relationship with your parent church, partner churches, or sending organizations can be difficult at times. Frustrations or confusion can come up on either side. It's worth spending time keeping things healthy, as much as it relies on you, not only for your own mental health, but for the potential fundraising. Most church plants are funded in part, or in whole, by parent churches, partner churches, or sending organizations. Finding a church that wants to support what you're doing can go a long way to helping you launch something that's sustainable.

Culture & Values

Culture is hard to define, and even harder to create. When you find a church culture that you love, it's far easier to duplicate it than it is to create it from scratch. This is one of the many benefits of having a parent church that resembles the one you hope to launch. With a little effort, you can carry the culture, values, and what makes it unique, with you. You can literally copy and paste the values from your parent church into your new board manual and use them in your visitor events and membership class.

The downside to this is obvious. It's very easy to duplicate an existing culture, which means our default will be to do more of what the church is already doing. Creating something new that reaches new people is far more difficult. This isn't an issue of either/or, but both/and. The church needs more healthy churches, so if you find one, duplicate it. But the church also needs more diverse churches, which will be easier to do if we have more healthy churches willing to embrace diverse ideas.

Connections

Out of the first 25 people to join our launch team, almost all of them came from our parent church or connections and friendships people had from there. A parent church that resembles the church you're launching can do a lot to send people or help a church planter connect with new people. The hardest part of building a church plant is gathering new people, so having a core group that already understands the vision and mission can make this process 100 times easier. In fact, having a parent church that is willing to send people or let you recruit people from its rolls who already understand what you're doing is more useful than financial donations or anything else. With enough of the right people, the new church can make up all the other areas on this list with ease.

Discipleship/Coaching

I learned not only how to preach to a younger audience, but how to hold membership classes, talk about giving, and help people grow in their faith from the example and teachings of our parent church and their pastor, Paul Risler. This goes beyond the discipleship process. When a church plant resembles the vision and mission of the parent church, it is far more common for the church planter to be mentored or discipled by the lead pastor. When a church planter is hired to do something new, or hired to reach new people, or launch a new kind of worship service, it is far more likely they will need to find emotional and spiritual support from someone who more closely understands the unique challenges of the kind of church they are launching.

Policy

Forming a board and operating with a set of policies is difficult, even if you have a template. If you're launching out of a healthy church, you can save time by adapting most of the policies you received from our parent church. Learning these things in an established church that resembles the culture, values, and organizational structure you hope to launch can save you years of work, headaches, and conflict.

Prayer & Support

Don't underestimate the power of people thinking and praying for us during this journey. This kind of encouragement can't be measured. The next chapter shares more about the importance of prayer.

Reflection Questions

1. When you consider the health/unhealth of your parent church or sending organization, where would you place them on the spectrum?
2. When you consider the values and practices of your parent church or sending organization, or the overarching accepted norms of your connection, how does this compare to the vision of your church plant? Are they similar or different?
3. Based on the answers to 1 and 2, what quadrant do you find yourself in?
    a. **Mentor**: What advice from your parent church has been the most helpful so far?
    b. **Advocate**: How might your parent church support you even if they don't always understand what you're doing? Be specific.
    c. **Mirror**: Are you trying to mirror what your parent church does without considering whether it's emotionally or spiritually healthy? We don't need more unhealthy churches. It's your job to break the cycle and embrace a new way of doing church.

d. **Antagonist**: Have you considered finding a different parent church or sending organization? If not, what other avenues of support can you find to help sustain you personally? What practices can you implement to ensure you don't get burnt out from the additional weight of unhealthy expectations? What is the bare minimum you need to interact with your parent church or sending organization without raising suspicion or causing additional harm?

	Healthy	Unhealthy
Similar	*Mentor*	*Mirror*
Different	*Advocate*	*Antagonist*

Church Planter's Toolkit

Go to churchplantershandbook.org to access the following resources related to this chapter:

- **Church & Nonprofit Sustainability Audit**: This simple Audit can show some of the strengths and weaknesses that could impact a parent church's relationship to a church plant.

Chapter 5

Prayer

One of the most important lessons I've ever learned about trusting God, I learned from my preaching professor, Rev. Dr. Joni Sancken.

We were taught to prepare a sermon using a simple method, common in seminaries. We would identify the problem in our passage of scripture, and what God was doing in the passage, and then explore a similar problem in our world, and what God was doing in the world about it.[1] In this model, our sermons could be summarized by a single sentence related to God's activity.

In these summary sentences, we were told to use strong action verbs.

Dr. Sancken would remind us, "Let God do the heavy lifting."

God *heals* the blind.
God *loves* everyone.
God *liberates* the oppressed.
God *plants* churches.

"Use strong action verbs."

Let God do the heavy lifting.

This is good news! You don't have to do the heavy lifting. You can be you, in all your glorious, natural limitations: limited in time, energy, and resources.

It's ok to be human. Receive this truth with a deep sense of relief. You don't have to be perfect, infallible, or all powerful.

You're allowed to have limits and fears and imperfections.

You're allowed to be human.

You're not only *allowed* but *required.* The first of the ten commandments is "thou shalt have no other gods before me," and this certainly includes you.

Prayer, at its most basic level, is an act of acknowledging that you're not God and that's ok.

God loves calling people to do things they can't do on their own because God isn't interested in simply watching you do things. God wants to be involved. God wants the task at hand to require trust and divine intervention. When God called Moses, he was quick to challenge God, listing his limitations. In the end, God gave him Aaron (Exodus 4:10-17), and later when the burden became too great, he sent the wisdom of Jethro (Exodus 18), who told Moses, "The work is too heavy for you; you cannot handle it alone" (Exodus 18:18).

This verse is great advice for a church planter. The work is too heavy for you; you cannot handle it alone.

We need God and other people to make this work, and prayer helps with both.

Building a prayer team is one way for people to come around you and show their support, whether members of your launch team, members from partner churches, or friends and family.

Never underestimate the power of knowing there are people cheering you on.

The Prayers of a Church Planter

Church planting is a monumental task—too difficult for one person to do alone. It will produce dark nights and overwhelming experiences. Prayer is essential to remind us of our need for God and others. Here are four common church planting prayers.

The first is the prayer of desperation.

Scripture is filled with cries of desperation, from fear of failure to being overrun by one's enemies. It's good and healthy to open your heart and let God know exactly how you feel.

In those times when you're feeling depressed, discouraged, and distraught, cry out to God. God often doesn't bring suffering to an end in the moment, as if God is some kind of vending machine where you put in your prayers and get a soda, but God can bring deliverance.

Lament can help you remember that God is near to the brokenhearted.

After a season of conflict, I tried to quit church and everything. My District Superintendent put me on 30-day renewal leave instead, and I spent the time depressed. This isn't an uncommon experience with church planters. I cried out to God for deliverance and for weeks everything kept getting worse—not better. I was ready to quit.

The day I decided to quit, I got up and walked to a local coffee shop. On my way, I decided I'd tell my District Superintendent I was going to quit. I had a meeting scheduled with him that afternoon, so I spent the walk rehearsing the meeting in my head. After I got my drink and breakfast and I continued to plan my resignation, something unexpected happened.

The staff from our church walked into the coffee shop. They had no idea I'd be there.

It had been a week since I stepped away and they decided it would be a good idea to get together and meet. My leave had happened suddenly, so I'm sure they had lots to figure out in my absence. For whatever reason, one of them recommended they meet over coffee, at this coffee shop, on that morning.

They came in as a group and saw me sitting with my breakfast. They walked over and chatted. They were so glad to see me. They were so concerned about me. They were kind and compassionate. They didn't complain about the mess I had left behind. They reassured me they would take care of things while I was away.

It was the shot of encouragement I needed. I didn't end up quitting that day, and it's entirely because my staff decided to meet at a random coffee shop at the same time I was.

In darkness, God will bring the light you need.

The second is the prayer for wisdom.

James says it like this:

> "If any of you lacks wisdom, let him ask of God, who gives to all liberally and without reproach, and it will be given to him." (James 1:5)

This is one of the few prayers God *promises* to answer. God might not heal everyone who is sick, fix every problem that comes our way, or meet our pain with miracles, but God promises to give you wisdom if you're willing to humble yourself enough to ask for it.

God's wisdom can provide the clarity we need in the 100 different decisions we make every day. James explains later in chapter 3 what this wisdom looks like:

> "The wisdom that comes from heaven is first of all pure; then peace-loving, considerate, submissive, full of mercy and good fruit, impartial and sincere." (James 3:17 NIV)

James is painting a picture of humility. When facing big decisions and complicated problems, taking time to humble yourself and ask for direction—from God and others—will always produce positive results. Quieting yourself, taking time to pray and then walking towards places of peace and clarity, provides the direction you might need in hard decisions.

Taking time to pray—time to center yourself and acknowledge your own humanness before a divine being—is also a great way to remind yourself that you're not God. Everyone has limitations. God isn't asking you to be superhuman. God is only ever asking that you be faithful—to take what you've been given and make something out of it (Matthew 25:14–30).

Take time daily to pause and reflect.

You're doing the best you can.

The third is prayers for breakthroughs.

With church planting, there are thousands of problems to solve and solutions to find. It's good and right to ask God for help in this. Church planting won't happen without God breaking through all the mundane barriers that keep new things from springing up in the world.

Back in seminary, I was able to take a class with Sue Nilson Kibbey, who is now the Director of the Bishop Bruce Ough Innovation Center at United Theological Seminary in Dayton, Ohio. At the time, she taught a leadership class, and after completing it, I spent the next two years as her teacher's assistant. If you know Sue, you know her heart and passion for breakthrough prayers.

Sue said this about how breakthrough prayers are helping churches reach new God-possibilities.

> The Church of Jesus Christ was never intended to be an inward-focused organization we are assigned to simply organize and administrate. Rather, according to Acts 2, it has always been intended to be a spiritual movement we unleash—through the power of collective prayer asking for God's next steps and new possibilities to break through—that miraculously transforms the mission field all around us.

When we began our plans for church planting, Sue invited Allyssa and me to share our thoughts on how breakthrough prayers impacted our church planting journey—a video that we've been told has been played in workshops and seminars for years now. Every time I hear about this video, I smile and nod but don't say much because I can't even remember what I said. It was seven years ago! Now, as I reflect on the importance of prayer in church planting, I thought it would be interesting to go check out what Allyssa and I had to say about prayer when we were getting started.

I went to YouTube and pulled up the video.

The first reaction I had was how young Allyssa and I looked. Seven years change you.

The second was the memory of how unhealthy we were during this time and how well we hide it on camera. We were stressed, young, struggling—in our marriage and in our ministry—and trying our best to hide it. We had a lot of growing up to do. Years of counseling and self-discovery would bring us to a place of emotional and spiritual health both as spouses and leaders. We also had a 9-month-old baby who was not sleeping through the night—and showing up to record a video on only a few hours of sleep isn't fun. But once I got past the cringe of our younger selves—a feeling I'm sure we can all relate to—I was able to listen to the words. We talked about how we trusted God to open the doors and prayed to find people and a location to launch this new church. We talked about how we needed God to show up—how it would be impossible without divine intervention.

In the end, this has remained true.

In fact, knowing how unhealthy and exhausted we were only proved that God did show up.

How else would things have worked out?

God loves meeting us in our weaknesses, for its then that God's grace can shine through.

That's the power of praying for breakthroughs.

"Thy will be done—without limitations!"

The church planter can't just sit back and pray, hoping it will all work out in the end because of faith (and if it didn't work out, then there must not have been enough faith!). Faith without works is dead (James 2:14-26). You should pray that God provides a location but also spend as much time as you can looking at local real estate websites, visiting every rental place you can. The secret to a breakthrough prayer is not only the prayer, but the willingness to do everything in your power to make your prayer a reality. Breakthrough prayers are all about petitioning God while also surrendering what you have to make it happen.

The last is a prayer of blessing.

Jeremiah says it clearly to the people of Israel while they were living in a foreign land.

> Also, seek the peace and prosperity of the city to which I have carried you into exile. Pray to the Lord for it, because if it prospers, you too will prosper. (Jeremiah 29:7 NIV)

God tells his people to pray for their communities, that if they prosper, so will God's people.

Many churches end their service with a benediction, but pastor Paul Risler often takes time to explain it. The service will be ending, and he'll come to the front, in a room full of people, all looking at him, declaring, "A benediction is a blessing. It's not a closing prayer. So, it's not something you do. It's something you receive. It's an act of grace. So, you don't close your eyes and bow your head, rather, you stare at me in the beady little eyes."

When we are out and about in our church planting communities, we're not just praying for our communities, we're walking with our eyes wide open, praying God's blessing over our communities, taking time to see those we encounter, seeing the needs, opportunities, and challenges.

A blessing requires us to see others as God sees them.

Don't underestimate the power of wanting good things for the people you're trying to serve. This posture can change our entire perspective on church planting.

> Growing Generous Givers
>
> Asking people to pray is an important part of fundraising in faith-based settings. If people take time to sincerely and prayerfully consider what they might give, it's between them and God what they do. In the end, you're not asking people of faith to give, as much as you're asking them to sincerely consider it or pray about it. This low-pressure, sincere request allows people to decide for themselves and is a way to soften the ask.

Prayer Booklet

Take time to remember that you need God's help. Ask God to bring the people you need to help carry this burden of the new church plant. Invite your team and anyone else to pray as well. Pray and seek good things for the place you've been sent to serve. Surround yourself with people who are willing to think positively about the work you're doing, and it will go a long way to keeping you encouraged on the journey.

To help you do this, we've developed a **Prayer Booklet** that covers many of the needs of new churches. This editable booklet can be used by yourself, your leaders, or your prayer team. Each devotion is meant to turn common fears and worries into statements of faith and assurance, helping the church planter and their team to increase their trust in the One who can do far more than we could ever think or imagine.

You can find this **Prayer Booklet** in the church planters toolkit at **churchplantershandbook.org/.**

Church Planter's Toolkit

Go to churchplantershandbook.org to access the following resources related to this chapter:

- **Prayer Booklet:** This collection of editable, original prayer devotions can be used by a church planter, launch team, or support staff.
- **Breakthrough Prayer Video:** In this short video, Allyssa and I share how prayer has had an impact on our church planting journey.

To access the Church Planter's Toolkit at churchplantershandbook.org,enter this passcode: PLANT!TOOLS

Part 2

Preparing the Launch

Chapter 6

Meeting New People

In Luke 10, Jesus gathers his disciples to send them out. He doesn't just gather the twelve, but over 70 disciples, representing men and women from all walks of life who had spent time with Jesus—enough time with Jesus that they were ready to go out and practice what they had learned.

The end goal of Jesus's teaching wasn't to stay on earth, caring for people all by himself. He intentionally and strategically invested in people who, in turn, could invest in others who could invest in others, and so forth. After the resurrection and ascension, Jesus deployed the church, and in time, the church would spread throughout the Roman Empire, as churches were planted in new places to reach new people.

Paul continues to be the most prolific example of this in the book of Acts: he would go to a city, connect with new people, find those interested in this new faith, and start meeting with them, until a church was born. We have seen this process play out over and over again throughout church history, but it all started with the example of Jesus in Luke 10.

Let's look at the instructions Jesus gives his disciples in Luke 10 and see what strategy emerges for meeting new people.

> "Go! I am sending you out like lambs among wolves. Do not take a purse or bag or sandals; and do not greet anyone on the road.
>
> "When you enter a house, first say, 'Peace to this house.' If someone who promotes peace is there, your peace will rest on them; if not, it will return to you. Stay there, eating and drinking whatever they give you, for the worker deserves his wages. Do not move around from house to house.
>
> "When you enter a town and are welcomed, eat what is offered to you. Heal the sick who are there and tell them, 'The kingdom of God has come near to you.'

> "But when you enter a town and are not welcomed, go into its streets and say, 'Even the dust of your town we wipe from our feet as a warning to you. Yet be sure of this: The kingdom of God has come near.'" (Luke 10:3-11)

"Peace" was a common greeting in the ancient world, but it was also infused with a deep theology of *shalom*, the Hebrew concept of wholeness and equity for all. In this passage, verse 6 can be more carefully translated "and if a child of peace lives there, your peace will rest upon them." In other words, to offer someone peace, and for them to receive it in this passage, carried more weight than a standard greeting. It meant they were an *off-spring* of peace—a person of peace—a product of God's new kingdom and shared Jesus's vision for the world. They were, at the very least, willing to play a part in bringing Jesus's vision of the world into reality. And according to Jesus, these people of peace were out there, just waiting to be invited.

That's what you're looking for in a launch team member. You're not trying to convince people to join your launch team, you're looking for the people who God has prepared ahead of time to join your launch team.

There are times in church history where the lessons here have been ignored, and the Christian faith has been forced or coerced onto people, no longer respecting the dignity of those who are hearing it for the first time. This has caused great harm and done more to hurt the cause of Jesus than to advance it. That is why these instructions are so important.

With this intention, Jesus sent his disciples out to the towns. They would share God's vision for *shalom*, and if the person reciprocated, they would add them to the ranks of Jesus's launch team.

This same principle can be used in recruiting launch team members. Share your vision, and if they are interested, invite them to join the launch team. Sounds simple, right? It kind of is, but doing this well is at the heart of what makes a new church work. If you have fewer than 50 people, all you have to offer is vision. Before a church grows, it's difficult to sustain programs, community, small groups, fresh expressions, or worship. It takes people to be a church. In the end, every church planter will need to develop a strategy for sharing their vision with as many people as possible and having a process for them to respond.

Growing Generous Givers

In the same way we must go out to meet people expecting to find someone who wants to support the vision, we should also ask people to give expecting them to want to. Here's what professional fundraisers and development staff know that the average church leader hasn't been told: **People want to be generous.** People are looking for a place to give. Not everyone, or every situation, but many people want to give. For many, the question isn't *whether* to give, but *where* they give. Why should they give to your church? What difference are you making? How are you going to use it? Are there robust processes in place to handle a large donation? Remind yourself that you're not trying to twist someone's arm into giving. Most people want to be generous and are looking for places to invest. All you're doing is extending an invitation, and the acceptance or rejection of that invitation shouldn't define your self-worth or your relationship with the person you invited.

Whatever the strategy, it starts with the same command: *Go.*

"Go. *I am sending you out like lambs among wolves.*"

To do this, you have to *go*—you have to leave the comfort of your home and meet new people.

"Go" is a simple command found throughout scripture. It is essential to the call narratives of Moses, Isaiah, and Jeremiah and to the Great Commission, "Go and make disciples…"

Go might be God's favorite command.

Yet, for every time God tells someone to "go," there are just as many examples of someone telling God "no."

In Luke 10, it's clear that this journey might be dangerous. While Jesus meant this in a more literal sense, as a neurodiverse introvert, anytime I leave my house with the intent to meet new people, it *feels* dangerous. Not to mention there are a thousand things vying for our attention, plenty to get distracted by, and lots of administrative work to keep us busy. There are hundreds of reasons church planters might struggle to go and meet new people. The two most common are *fear of rejection* and *unrealistic expectations.*

Fear of Rejection

When heading out the front door, with the hopes to meet new people, it's easy to worry that they won't be interested—that they might be annoyed. Years ago, when I first started church planting, this fear sat in me as if the middle-school version of myself still took up residence in my heart. You might struggle with this as well. This fear is nothing to be embarrassed by for its rooted in a truly healthy and normal need: fear of rejection is rooted in our need for belonging.

Acceptance and belonging are among the most basic human needs. Without them, we struggle to live whole and healthy lives. Acceptance and belonging are so essential to our mental health that it's no surprise that the fear of rejection is powerful in an equal and opposite direction.

While easy to understand, the solution is hard to live into. You have to flip this fear upside down: You're not going out to ask people to accept you, so get that idea out of your head. This isn't about you. There's no doubt that when someone chooses not to be a part of our churches, it *feels* personal, but this feeling has to be named and rejected.

Sit with this statement before moving on: Your sense of belonging can't come from the new people you're trying to gather.

This is why it's important for a church planter, or any pastor, to have a community outside the church. Authentic relationships and authentic belonging can give room for the pastor to go out and invite new people to be a part of the church without placing their own need of belonging on the shoulders of strangers.

When fear of rejection keeps you from asking someone to check out your church, what you're really saying is that this person—a stranger—holds the power to give you the belonging you need. They don't and it would be unreasonable to place this burden on them. You're not asking them to accept you; you're asking them to be a part of the unique mission God has called your church to—and if it's not for them, no harm done.

Your church might be hospitable to everyone, but it won't be for everyone. Allow someone to say "no thanks" to your church's mission without feeling like they are rejecting you personally.

Your goal isn't to convince anyone of anything. God isn't asking you to win, convert, or convince people to join your church. This is what's so brilliant about Jesus's instructions here. Jesus invites you to go out and find people *who have already been prepared to join this mission.*

To do this, you will need to talk to a lot of people, knowing that not everyone will fit into what God is doing in and through us. Of course they won't! Certainly, God is doing more in the world than what God is doing through you, *right*? If someone isn't the right fit for your new church, that's ok.

God has other plans for them.

> Growing Generous Givers
>
> The most common excuse we can come up with for not asking people to give (or do anything) is the fear they won't want to. We can tell ourselves "They won't want to do that" or "that's not how it works" or "they are too busy" or "they can't afford this." Don't let these thoughts guide your decisions. Remember, people are able to make their own decisions. *Don't make it for them.* They are allowed to say "no," but they won't be given the chance to say "yes" if you don't *ask*. Trust people enough to let them respond for themselves.

The best way to get an honest "yes" from someone is to let them say "no." It's very hard to ask someone for something when you *need* them to say yes. Needing a specific answer can create unnecessary tension and conflict in the conversation, making someone feel like saying no is going to hurt your relationship. Let go of these expectations and allow people to be honest.

In a way, there's a strange irony in how this fully inverts our fear of rejection. "Allowing" people to say "no" means you can continue being friendly with them afterwards. In this backwards sort of way, people who say no can still be People of peace, in that you can remain friendly, without hard feelings. And this allows you to more easily move on from a "no."

Most people you talk to won't be the people God has prepared for you. Move on and don't carry their "no" with you, or as Jesus said, "Shake the dust off your feet" (Matthew 10:14).

Unspoken Expectations

In a fairy tale many church planters tell, a good planter will be able spark a conversation with a random stranger, and by the end of the conversation, the stranger wants to get baptized. They can strut into town, bump into random strangers, chat them up, and naturally the conversation would lead to the church plant. They would ask questions, and in the end, they'd come to church, and the next thing you know, they have a full church!

But this is nothing more than a fairy tale. This is not how church planting or community organizing works.

This kind of pressure does far more to keep church planters from meeting new people than anything else. Unhealthy expectations will rob you of one of the most valuable resources you have as a church planter: your energy and confidence. If something is killing your confidence, you need to do a deep dive and figure out why. Usually, it's because of unspoken expectations that are either unreasonable, a bad fit for your gifting, or downright unhealthy.

In this fairy tale, only the truly charismatic, extroverts can plant churches. This is a story that is not only unhealthy, but untrue. You can struggle with small talk, find large crowds overwhelming, and be an introvert and still be called to plant a thriving church. Here's how.

Removing the Mystery

When I was little, my brother showed me a magic trick: After a few false reveals, my card would "magically" appear in my hand. It was amazing, and I had to know how it was done. Every time he did it for me, I'd beg him to show me how it worked, and he'd tell me it was something he learned in prison—a dark magic that he didn't want me to have to mess with.

I was twelve, what did I know about such things? Maybe he did learn dark magic in prison!

Turns out that wasn't the case.

In the end, he showed me how to do the trick and there is zero dark magic involved.

It's simple and requires almost no skill. I've used it dozens of times to impress my friends.

That's the thing about magic tricks. They are amazing and mind-blowing, until you know how they are done. They are often very simple.

For me, meeting new people and inviting them to join a new church felt like a magic trick—something that I saw other people do, and it must have been some kind of magic that made it work, because how would that ever happen?

Turns out it's simple and requires very little skill, and people have been doing it for generations.

They say a magician never reveals its secrets, but I'm not a magician and what I'm going to share in this chapter isn't a secret, and to be clear, I'm certainly not suggesting you trick anyone. I'm merely suggesting that for those who feel there's a big secret to reaching new people and building a launch team, it's not that complicated.

The way something is done is often less impressive than the results. We're all living in Oz, and when we pull back the curtain, the wizard is just an ordinary insecure dude like the rest of us. Some will read this chapter and feel that way—disappointed it isn't more complicated. For others, you will be glad and take a deep sigh of relief, taking something as mysterious as reaching new people and breaking it down into simple steps that remove the mystery. For others, it will be a confirmation or reminder of what you already know.

This model blends some basic practices of church planting with community organizing. Community organizing is a process that involves people working together to address issues that affect their community with the hope to produce change.[1] A new church start, set on making the world a better place, has to take the best practices of church planting and blend them with the best practices of community organizing.

Here it is, in three simple steps.

Step 1. Prepare the Vision Documents

A lot of work needs to go into ensuring your vision is clear to ensure people accept or reject it accurately. With that initial vision clarified and developed, put together three key documents.

A "one-pager."

This is a color, printed, single page that lays out the vision for this new church, laying it out in a visually appealing way. Having a document to hand a potential launch team member makes it easier to explain it to them.

A one-pager should include the following:

What: Logo of church and church's mission statement

Where: Photos of the location or a map showing the location.

Who: This should include photos of current launch team members and/or pastors. Avoid stock photos. If you don't have a good picture of the people you're hoping to connect with, leave this out. For some traditions, a photo of the church planter might be appropriate. For others, it might not be. Know your audience.

Why: A summary of the vision.

When: A timeline for the launch or overall plan.

How: A brief explanation of your strategy.

A response card.

This included all the ways that someone could respond, often categorized by the commitment.

A spreadsheet to track who we were meeting with.

This would include their names, contact information, meeting dates, notes on the meeting, and a column for each of these responses. This allows you to keep track of the dozens of people you will meet with.

With these three documents, you have what you need to start meeting new people.

Step 2. Schedule the Meeting

Most people hate door-to-door salespeople. They come to your door, and it feels impossible to get them to leave without closing the door on them, no matter how assertive and nice you are.

Don't be a door-to-door salesperson.

No one should feel pressured into a conversation that they don't want. This is one benefit of reaching out to people and scheduling a time to meet or meeting them at an event designed for networking. People are far more comfortable in conversations when they know what to expect.

Have you ever received a text from someone saying, "We need to talk"? These ambiguous messages are anxiety producing! Knowing the purpose of a conversation is an essential part of effective communication. So, when reaching out, always tell them why, tailoring each message for each person. Consider connecting with categories of people:

> *First*, reach out to **people you want to invite to be a part of the launch team**. For them, let them know you're planting a church and ask if you could talk about it.
>
> *Second*, reach out to people who are **stakeholders and leaders in the wider community or city.** For them, make it clear that you want to get their perspective on the wider community and share your heart for planting a church that wants to engage in local concerns. Say something like, "We're trying to learn as much about the neighborhood as possible and would love to hear your thoughts on what makes this a great place to live or work." Asking people sincerely for their opinion opens the doors to all kinds of wonderful conversations and relationships.
>
> *Third*, reach out to **people who attend other churches**, either as leaders or members. Treat this group similar to the community leaders, letting them know that you want to learn more about the needs of the wider community, but include a few other topics. For example, ask them to pray for you, to be a partner church in some kind of shared, community effort. They might also be

willing to make recommendations for people we might connect with. Church people often have friends looking for a church, but for whatever reason, aren't interested in their friend's church. For example, they might have a friend who is gay, who wouldn't be accepted at their home church, and they think they might fit well in yours. People are often eager to make introductions if they think the new church might meet a need.

You might consider reaching out to people from the following areas:

Parent Churches: The great thing about having a parent church is having a list of people you can invite to join you. If you have a parent church or you're launching a satellite campus, this is a great place to meet potential launch team members. The only concern is to make sure they are dedicated to radical hospitality and learn to avoid too much insider language.

Partner Churches: If you can build relationships with churches willing to partner with you, they might give you permission to work with people in their congregation. For example, they might have extra media, children's ministry, or worship volunteers they can "loan out" for a season to help you get started. While many churches will say "no" it's worth putting yourself out there and asking.

Launch Team Members: Your current launch team members will be your biggest asset to connecting with new people. Ask them to brainstorm people you could reach out to and teach them about the importance of connecting with new people. Those who are newest to your launch team or church are the ones with the best connections. Get to know them and see how they might be willing to introduce you to. *You can find a handout in the church planter's toolkit to help key leaders think about who they might invite in the "Help Us Meet New People" handout.*

Networking Events: Participate in every possible networking event in your neighborhood. This might include things like Chambers of Commerce, Rotary, Nonprofit Collaboratives, Block Parties, Art Walks, Area Commissions, PTAs, etc. When possible, volunteer to lead or help with events. You will meet more people volunteering and planning an event than attending one.

Community Leaders: Reach out to and meet with as many local leaders as you have time. This might include the local mayor, police chief, fire chief, city council member, area commissioner, etc. This is a great chance to meet influencers and share your vision for being a positive asset in their community. As you hear their vision for the community and the unique needs, begin to dream with your community partners how you might join them in making a positive difference.

For those you're interested in joining the launch team, try to meet in their homes or invite them over to yours. There is something special about sharing space in someone's home. When that doesn't work, meet with them over lunch, or at a coffee shop. For community leaders and stakeholders, offer to meet them wherever is most convenient.

For potential launch team members, you can meet people one-on-one, as a family, or in larger gatherings. For a new church start disconnected from a parent church, it might be a lot of one-on-one meetings. This is because the people you're trying to connect with don't know each other already. For a satellite church, or church-within-a-church, larger groups might work just as well and even help build momentum, because people know each other.

Whenever you get a meeting scheduled, you'll be able to go, with everyone knowing what to expect. This is a way of knocking on people's doors in cultures where door-to-door solicitation is frowned upon.

Step 3. Hold the Conversation

The meeting is set, and you walk into their office, enter their foyer, find your seat at the restaurant, or invite them into your living room. Once you've settled in—maybe you passed out the iPads to distract the kids, or the food has arrived—start the conversation.

Jesus's instructions in Luke 10 tell those he's sending out *exactly* what to say. Having a plan continues to be good advice. Structuring a presentation or conversation in an intentional way will often produce intentional results.

We've all been in far too many meetings with awkward silences, unclear expectations, small talk that gets off topic, or any of a dozen other things that derail conversations to know it's important to go in with a plan. You should try to come up with a plan that works for you, considering your communications style and goals. Here is one strategy. It's adapted from various fundraising endeavors—including raising personal support and capital improvement campaigns—but could be used in a variety of ways including community organizing, church planting, and more.

Here it is, broken down into six stages:

Small Talk

For those neurotypicals reading, you might find it hilarious this step is included, but it's important, nonetheless. This is more than just small talk. Take time to be curious about the people you are meeting. Get to know them. This isn't a transaction. This is an opportunity to build new relationships that could have a lasting impact on your church and community. Treat each encounter as a divine encounter, where you get to meet the very image of God in another person. What are they passionate about? What do they care about? How are they hurting? Don't linger on this step too long, but don't skip over it either.

Share Your Story

After this, transition to share your story of wanting to plant a church and your hopes of being a blessing in the community. People connect with stories better than they do anything else, so practice sharing your story of becoming a church planter, or why you're planting this specific church, or why you're planting in this specific location. It's good to practice this ahead of time and get used to repeating it. Don't write a novel. Keep it short and concise but be sure to make it authentic and compelling.

Share the Vision & Strategy

This would often transition naturally to our vision for the church plant. At this moment, hand out the one-pager and walk through the *who, what, where, why,* and *how* of planting the church, tailoring the presentation to the unique perspective of each person. This should briefly include your plan and strategy. People are more likely to be a part of something new if they can sense you have thought through the steps needed to do it.

Ask Questions & Get Input

Now that you've shared your story, vision, and strategy, take time to sit back and listen.

Whenever and wherever you hold a conversation like this, whether one-on-one or in a group, allow those present to engage in the conversation. This time together is as much about them, what they have to offer, and what they hope to see, as it is about your church plant. Take time to listen.

Discussion needs to be tailored to each person, depending on whether they are a potential launch team member, community leader, or partner church. In all of these cases, ask a couple of simple questions similar to the ones below.

> What's great about this community/city/neighborhood?
> What are some of the needs of this community/city/neighborhood?
> What do you think a great church in this community would look like?

The questions should make sense for your planting stage, what you're trying to find out, and what the person or group might have thoughts about. This gives people a chance to process your vision and connect it to what they know, love, and are concerned about in their community.

If their answers directly relate to your vision, take time to validate that.

When possible, go in ready to listen and get people's advice. It is the best kept secret to gaining trust and clarifying God's vision for the church, and it will produce amazing results.

I met Allie at a chamber meeting, and we exchanged business cards. She was currently working as a financial advisor. A few months later, our church launched, and we were in the middle of a sermon series on giving. I was looking for input on how people are uncomfortable talking about money and I remembered Allie. I dug out her business card and called her, asking her some questions related to the sermon, people's feelings about money, and what advice she had. She gave me great talking points for my sermon and seemed honored I had asked for her advice. That week, curious about what I was going to say, she visited our church for the first time.

Then, she and her boyfriend started attending.

A few years later, I officiated their wedding.

They have been a part of our church ever since.

Seeking people's advice is one of the best ways for building positive relationships. You're not trying fill up an auditorium with warm bodies. You're taking time to get to know real people, with real needs and unique personalities. You have a chance to learn about people's gifts and passions and talents and even dream a little of how they might be able to partner with you to change the world. Going into a conversation sincerely and authentically curious and interested in learning more about somebody goes a long way to keeping this whole thing from feeling like some kind of icky sales pitch.

Offer a Way to Respond

If you want to stay at someone's house, like Jesus instructed his disciples, you have to knock on their door and ask them. The same is true for church plants—or anything really.

To find out if someone is willing to give a part of themselves to this new church, **you have to ask.** If you do everything else in this chapter perfectly but refuse to offer an opportunity for people to respond, you might meet a lot of great people and even make some wonderful memories, but it's unlikely your church or community efforts will turn into anything substantial.

You have to ask, and it needs to be clear. Change in your community and growth in your church will happen when you ask people to play a specific role in making it a reality.

In the ancient world, before the hospitality industry, neighbors would open their doors to travelers. Having people stay in your home costs you. It means giving up your space, food, time, and energy to make sure they feel welcomed and comfortable.

While potential launch team members might not provide you a place to stay, they should be willing to offer hospitality to God's vision for this new church or community effort. In other words, they need to be willing to give up their time, energy, resources, and talents to make room for this new vision God is bringing into the world.

They are willing for the vision to cost them.

The only way you will know if they are willing to contribute to this vision is if there is a moment when you ask them.

There's something that happens in the hearts and minds of someone when they are asked to help. They might love what you're doing, enjoy hearing the stories, and support your vision, but until you turn it around and ask them to play a part in it, there's a good chance they haven't considered that they could be a part of it. Taking time to do everything else laid out in this chapter, but failing to ask, is the easiest mistake you can make.

As Jesus said: "Ask and it will be given to you; seek and you will find; knock and the door will be opened to you" (Matthew 7:7 NIV).

This is one of the most important lessons in doing anything new. You might not get everything you ask for, but you'll rarely get what you don't ask for.

Here's an easy way to push through the fear of the ask and make it as painless as possible.

First, let them say no. Don't hang your relationship on their response.

Second, lay out different ways for people to respond and let them pick one.

For a launch team, you might consider having a response card that includes a variety of possible responses. Here are some examples:

- **E-Newsletter:** When possible, get as many people as you on your email list. This way, if they weren't interested now, or the current iteration of the church, they might like what you're doing later on and check you out. If someone is in any way interested in what you're doing, ask them if you can add them to your e-newsletter. Don't leave them to go and sign up later. If they are interested, get their email and add them yourself.
- **Pray**: People of faith, regardless of what church they go to, can take time to pray for you. This is the least someone can do if they lead or attend another church.
- **Give**: Growing generous givers needs to be a part of every step of the process, including here. Be clear right from the start that you are hoping launch team members and supporters will start giving

as soon as they can. Offer this as a legitimate and meaningful way for them to support God's vision for a new church. Don't apologize for needing financial support. Everyone who is doing anything in the world worth anything has had to ask people or institutions to financially support them.

- **Serve**: To launch a church, you will need volunteers, small group leaders, children's ministry leaders, and more. Being on the launch team means committing to serving in some way. Listen to their stories and feedback and find a way to name the gifts and talents they have that would help make this vision a reality.
- **Join the launch team**: Have a place for them to commit to the launch team at a level they are comfortable with. Consider creating multiple levels of membership: those who want to commit for the next few months leading up to the launch and those who are making a year-long commitment. The idea here is that there are some who want to support your church, but plan to go back to their current church once it has launched. Statistically, the majority of the people who help you launch won't be at the church five years later. By giving room for this at the beginning, you can avoid hurt feelings on both sides.

All in all, hope they say "yes" to one or more of the responses you provide. They might also want to think and pray about it. Never force them to decide right there. If they're ready to respond, it will be clear. I remember one conversation where we did this, and the husband told us after the conversation that they would think and pray about. The wife interrupted and said, "No, we're on board. We're joining the launch team." She was ready. They went on to be one of our biggest givers and servant leaders the first five years of our church plant.

For everyone who is on the fence, or not sure, leave the conversation open. Leave the response card with them and let them know you will reach out to them after they've had time to think about it.

Through all of this, you want to contextualize the conversation to what you know about the person or what you learn about them. Learn to read the room.

If they open up about how much church has hurt them, and they're not sure about whether they even believe in God, spend time talking about that. You can, of course, explain how you hope to do things differently in your new church. Or you could spend most of the time asking them how they wish church could be different. It's your job as the leader to get to know the people you're meeting with and responding to them in a way that makes sense. Receive the conversations with grace, trusting God, and refraining from becoming defensive or taking their response or critiques personally.

Small Talk—Again

Go back to something you heard them tell you at the beginning. You want them to know that you care about them as a person and you're not just meeting with them to get something out of them. This isn't a sales pitch. It's an invitation. Don't take the time to meet with someone if you're not actually interested in who they are as a person.

If framed with positivity and hope, this can go well, strengthen friendships, honor people's dignity of choice, and bring God's kingdom near—even if they don't want to be on your launch team.

This same structure can be used hundreds of different ways.

Context Matters

Depending on who you meet with, you will want to adjust this conversation accordingly.

Here are a few examples of how you might spread the conversation out and adapt according to the audience. To start, let's look at a conversation with a potential launch team member. If they don't clearly fit into any other category or have expressed any level of interest in the church plant, they are potential launch team members.

Potential Launch Team Member

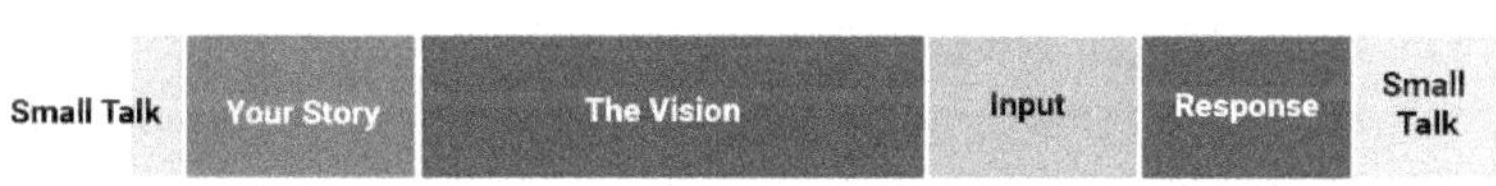

In this scenario, most of the time will be spent sharing your story and the vision for this new church plant. Of course, you still have time to get input but you're setting aside an equal amount of time to go over, in detail, the various ways they can respond.

Look how this is different from a conversation with a community leader:

Community Leader

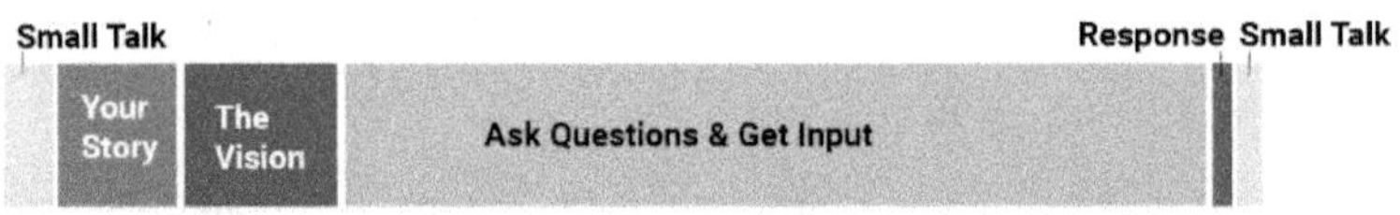

You can see, the time spent on your story and vision is cut dramatically. Unless they ask to know more, there's no need to share more than a brief overview and focus on the parts of your vision that they would be most interested in, like how your church might benefit the neighborhood. Most of the time is spent asking questions and getting their input. You've arranged the meeting to learn more about the community, so go in with great questions and look for ways your church can support the good already happening in the community. When they mention community groups or organizations that share a similar vision or DNA, thank them and promise to look into them. Then, look at the response. It is negligent. At best, you might ask them to connect you with someone they mentioned or make some kind of introduction. You can invite them to visit on a Sunday, but you're not obligated to, unless it makes sense. You don't want this to feel like a bait-and-switch. Stick to the purpose you set the meeting for. You will also notice that small talk is also shortened at the beginning and end. I've found that government leaders and neighborhood stakeholders are often busy and don't have time for more than a few moments of polite small talk. But once again, read the room and go in prepared. There are some community leaders who are looking for a reason to talk about their kids or favorite football team.

Now, consider how it might look for a church leader or member of another church:

Church Member/Leader

It's like a potential launch team member, but you're not spending as much time on your vision and story. While it's similar to a community leader, you do go in with specific requests, which might include prayer, financial support, volunteers, or partnership. Recruiting partner churches is a great way to build a launch team and find essential leaders early in the process. It's also great to find like-minded churches that you can partner with in community endeavors. Be sure to ask any significant church leaders what they are doing in the community and ways your church can get involved. Churches are often threatened by church plants "moving into the neighborhood, when we've been here for years!" Disarm this critique by offering to support what is already happening.

And finally, here is what it would look like adjusted for a financial giving campaign:

Fundraising Campaign

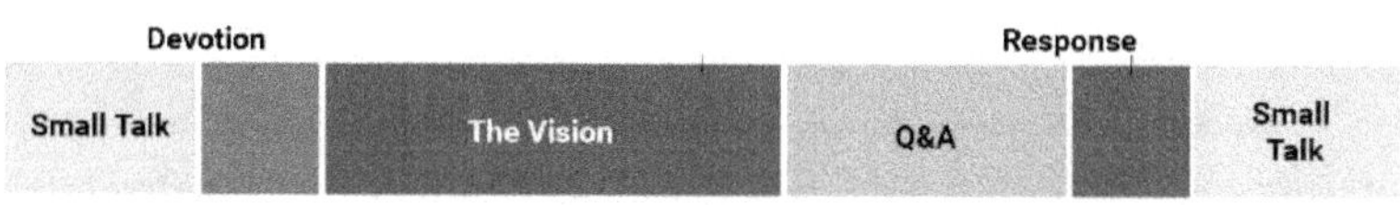

This can be used in a group setting, made up of stakeholders in your church or a launch team member. Often, fundraising campaigns are used with people who are already committed to your church. Because of this, give plenty of time for small talk and hanging out before and after the presentation. You can accompany this time with food and drinks to help people feel relaxed. Then, instead of sharing our story (since they are all stakeholders and know you already), share a brief devotion that connects to the ask you're going to make. After that, go through the one-pager and share your vision and strategy for the campaign. When it comes to getting input, instead of asking them questions, open it up for questions. By the time you've gathered stakeholders, the plan has likely been well established and approved by your leadership team, so you're not looking for input as much as questions that help bring clarity. Finally, the response: in this case, the invitation to either make a pledge, donation, or pray about making a pledge/donation, depending on when this takes place in the timeline. Learning how to do this will give you a significant head start on fundraising.

This method isn't the only way to accomplish the task of meeting new people, just like my brother's card trick isn't the only card trick out there, but it's an example of how you can remove the mystery of connecting with new people and take intentional steps towards building a launch team.

Don't Get Discouraged.

Here's the truth: not everyone you talk to will want to be part of your church.

The fear of rejection isn't overcome by convincing yourself that people won't reject you—they will. Instead, the fear of rejection is overcome by coming to a place where their rejection doesn't impact your identity. This is why it's so important to do the hard work of self-reflection before you begin this.

The only way you will find your People of Peace is by talking with as many people as you can.

Rev. Amy Aspey, a UMC church planter, launched Short North Church in Columbus, Ohio, around the same time as Central City Church. She's a master at networking, meeting new people, and building positive relationships with people in the community. She shared these tips recently with our conference's Greenhouse class, and are worth taking to heart:

> **1. Be prepared to invest time, regularly.** Networking takes a TON of time. I had coffee or a meal with every blessed person who would meet with me. I averaged about 30 people a month. For the most part, people are not going to come to you, so you have to figure out a way to go to the people. It's critical to make space for networking every week. Networking is an *over and over and over again* thing because relationships are built over time and ministry is never done.

2. **Be interested in people and LISTEN more than you talk.** Ask questions about what interests whomever you are talking with.

3. **Be intentional about follow-up.** Follow-up can look like information, an invitation, a connection, an offer to help, and/or a concern that was shared.

Bonus Tips: Be yourself. And remember that your belovedness as a child of God isn't tied to any outcome—success or failure. Worth can get connected to results and that's dangerous, whether things are wildly successful or falling apart. God loves you, period.

Sowing Seeds

In Matthew 13, Jesus told a story of a guy who throws out seeds on all kinds of grounds: some are swallowed up by weeds, others fall on paths, but some fall on "good soil."

This parable reveals that *the quality of the soil* doesn't determine *the value of the farmer*.

People who like to control things would tell the farmer to be more careful. "Stop sowing seeds in bad soil!" If the farmer wants to plant a garden right, they should prepare the soil, remove the weeds, and not waste any seeds by throwing them on the path. *Why is the farmer throwing seeds on the path anyways?!* When the passage is read this way, the point is missed.

The point isn't to worry about which seeds will grow, but to toss them anywhere you can, and here's why. Fun fact: Jesus isn't actually talking about gardening

Jesus is talking about humans. And unlike soil, humans are much harder to understand. A farmer can see where the path is and where the good soil is. A church planter would be foolish to assume they can read people that well.

Consider the story Jesus tells of the two brothers. Their father asks them to help with some work. One says "yes!" enthusiastically but never shows up. The other says "no," but over time, he regrets his decision and shows up anyway. Do you think you will be a better judge of someone's readiness than a parent is of their child?

The people you think are going to be amazing assets to your church plant might end up checking out within a month. Others who seem hesitant might become significant leaders.

We had a family that started visiting our church right after we launched, but after chatting with them, they informed us they were visiting lots of churches—and weren't sure where they were going to land. They were hesitant to meet with my wife and me, but eventually we got a date on the calendar for dinner where we shared our vision for this new church and let them ask questions. They were supportive but clearly hesitant and were not ready to make any commitments. We gave them the space they needed.

I didn't leave their house *shaking off the dust* and calling down God's judgment on them, as Luke suggests, and I'm glad I didn't.

Over time, they settled on our church and attended regularly.

Then they started serving.

Then, the mother of the family, Molly Rule, became our children's director and easily one of the most influential and important staff members in our church, caring for our children's ministry through difficult seasons, including COVID and a church merger.

If I had taken their hesitancy personally, let my feelings be hurt, or called down God's judgment on them for not giving me a solid *yes* at the beginning, I'm confident they would have found somewhere else to attend.

Let me say it again: Church planters are often terrible judges of "good soil."

Put *the ask* out and let it land where it does. God will take care of the rest.

Those you think will become committed to a new endeavor, might leave before things get started. And others you would have never considered, might become significant leaders. Those who don't seem excited, might give generously and offer wisdom in times of trouble, while those who light up at the first meeting might go on and on about how much they love our church, only to turn out to be dangerous and toxic. It's hard to know what will produce fruit that will last, so the best you can do is to be patient, loving, offer grace to everyone as you journey together, and avoid getting distracted by those who seem overly excited. Our egos love to be around people who celebrate our ideas, but these interactions are nothing more than shiny objects distracting us from what matters. Don't get distracted by shiny compliments. Judge people on what they do over a long period of time, not how they react the first time they hear an idea.

And whatever you do, don't give up.

Good News

Can I share with you some of the best news a church planter can hear? It's pretty simple, but if you take adequate time to ponder it and let it sink into your soul, you will find great comfort in these words: **If God is calling you, God is also calling people to join you.**

Let that sink in.

To be clear, this doesn't mean you should subscribe to the "name it and claim it" theology, but if God is calling you somewhere, God already has People of Peace waiting for you.

That doesn't mean it will be easy. Many people you talk to will not want to be a part of your church. Others who join the launch team will move on to other churches. But if God is sending you—if the God who is able to do far more than you could ever think or imagine put the effort into preparing you and giving you a call to start something new—surely God has done the same for those you need to make it happen.

They might be difficult to work with, or say *no* at first, or challenge your ideas, or any of a number of other things people do when they are in a community together—but they are there.

They might be less than you want.

They might be different than you expect.

But they are there.

Do you remember Jesus's parable of the banquet in Luke 14?

A wealthy leader made plans for a great banquet and of course, he sent invitations to all of his friends, family, and acquaintances to join him. Yet, on the day of the banquet, no one comes.

They are all too busy.

If you're a church planter who is trying to build a launch team and it's all smaller than you want, then you know how this feels. If you've ever planned an event that no one came to, you know how that feels. You're not alone. In this story, we read that "The owner of the house became angry" (Luke 14:21). This is the biggest party he has ever thrown, and the people he loves and knows well don't want anything to do with it?

Can you imagine how that would feel?

He was angry. You might get angry too.

This parable teaches a hard truth: Your friends and family may or may not want to be a part of your big day; it doesn't matter how much work you put into it, how early the invitations go out, or how important it is to you. The people you want to be a part of the church might not be the people God has in mind. Church planters are often discouraged and even angry about this. They launched a church with specific people in mind only to find those people aren't interested.

For many, they might be tempted to give up and write it off as a failure. Or they might change the date and time, hoping to make it work for those they want there. This is only logical. If you are planning something as important as a church, you will cater to the people you want to be there.

But if we do that, we've missed the point of this parable.

This man could have been tempted to move the date, location, or order of the events in the hope that he might be able to accommodate those he wants there. But Jesus has him do something different.

After being rejected by his *target audience,* the man tells his *launch team* to, "Go out to the roads and country lanes and compel them to come in, so that my house will be full."

Or as Jesus says moments before this story:

> "But when you give a banquet, invite the poor, the crippled, the lame, the blind, and you will be blessed. Although they cannot repay you, you will be repaid at the resurrection of the righteous." (Luke 14:13 NIV)

Are you struggling to connect with people? Is it possible that you're too distracted trying to invite people *like you* or people *you like*?

What if God has someone else in mind?

What if God called you to plant a church for people you haven't met yet, who aren't like you, and who need a church more than you could imagine?

Back in high school, when we launched a youth center, my brother, after getting out of prison, prayed that God would "send the kids no one else wants."

There was a United Methodist church planter who was doing great work with people in recovery, but when people referred to it as a "recovery church," the church planter looked annoyed. They were afraid of calling it that might push other people away—people uncomfortable being around people in recovery. Over time, they couldn't avoid the fact that they were connecting well with people in recovery, and over time they learned to celebrate that. A year later, they announced to their leadership team they were going to focus even more energy on serving people in recovery.

It was unavoidable—they had found their People of Peace.

Love the people who show up, not the ones you wish showed up.

Trusting that God has someone in mind is a step of faith that every church planter must take. We go out, knowing that someone will want to be a part of what we do. As we see in the Wesleyan faith, God's grace is working in the world, in everyone's life, at all times, and in all places, and so you can trust that some of those people are being prepared to be a part of what God is asking of you. This changes how we approach evangelism, outreach, meeting new people, and it changes how we set, and approach church planting goals related to these things.

Input & Output Goals

My wife, who is also a church planter, once told me:

> Ideas are not vision. We can come up with ideas all day long, but vision is seeing who God is calling you to be or do and move towards that.

You might want to become a church of 200 people and have lots of great ideas of what it could look like but *wanting it* doesn't get you any closer to *having it.*

This has led to another great lesson in church planting and church leadership in general. We must learn the difference between *input* and *output* goals.

Consider this passage in 1 Corinthians:

> I planted the seed, Apollos watered it, but God has been making it grow. (1 Corinthians 3:6)

Paul is explaining how the credit shouldn't go to him or Apollos, for its God who is doing the real work. *Paul planted, Apollos watered, but God is the one who makes it grow.* There are some things you can do (input) but you can rarely control the outcome (output).

> **Input goals** are the things we can do; the stuff we can put effort into. They include everything in our circle of control and influence.
>
> **Output goals** are the results, or what we get out of it.

Input goals include planting and watering. Output goals include the plant growing and producing fruit. We can control one, but not the other.

This past spring, my son and I planted a few seeds in our little urban garden. We prepared the soil, watered it, but we had no control over whether those seeds grew. In fact, I laid a whole line of zucchini and only one plant sprung up out of the entire row. I knew better than to spend my time worrying about the seeds that didn't grow. All of my attention went into the one that did grow!

Don't waste your time trying to get the seeds that didn't grow to sprout when you could be tending to the ones that did.

Jim Collins, in his monograph *Good to Great and the Social Sectors,* explains it like this:

> The confusion between inputs and outputs stems from one of the primary differences between business and social sectors. In business, money is both an input (a resource for achieving greatness) *and* an

> output (a measure of greatness). In the social sectors, money is *only* an input, and not a measure of greatness.[2]

In church planting, money is never a measure of greatness. Wealthy churches are not the goal in starting a new church—increased connectional giving, larger salaries, or fancy buildings should never be the goal. Money is not a good output goal, but it is a necessary input. Studies show that the more funding used to start a church, the larger it will be. Money (input) influences attendance (output).[3]

Yet, money isn't the *only* input required, and attendance isn't the *only* output to measure. Collins suggests the best measure of output is *impact*. Attendance is just one way to measure impact, and it might not be the best. For example, Jesus's teachings on the Eucharist in the Gospel of John did a lot to hurt his attendance, while overall, increasing the impact of his mission. Output goals in church are more nuanced than attendance. Yet, at the same time, to suggest attendance doesn't matter is to gloss over the sorrow and regret a church planter feels when they open worship services only to see an empty room. Attendance can't be the final output goal, but it's hard to make dents on any other output goals without first reaching this one. While the final output goal should include overall impact—things like transformed lives and communities—the goal of this chapter is to help you find the people who will help you reach those goals.

Here's how input and output goals impact meeting new people.

You can make a goal of meeting 100 people, but you can't control how many of those will want to be a part of your church—no matter how charismatic you are, how talented, or prepared or how great your vision is, you have zero control on who makes a commitment to our launch team. In fact, *if you had control*—and you found some way to trick or force people into being on the launch team—you have a bigger problem. Take comfort in knowing you aren't trying to control who says "yes." People can make their own decisions; this is a good thing.

Instead of pretending like you can control what people do, you must remain focused on *what you can control*, by setting reasonable, manageable input goals.

Here are some examples of output goals that can cause people to freeze up and corresponding input goals that might help you get unstuck.

Output Goal: *I need 50 people to join the launch team.*

This hope is great, but it does nothing to help you move in this direction. In fact, it can do the opposite. As your deadlines approach, this hope can turn to despair, and you might no longer have the energy to get off the couch, or out of the office, and meet new people. Instead, input goals can give you actionable items. Consider these alternative input goals.

Input Goals: *Invite 150 people to chat: email 100, text at least 50, and invite no fewer than 20 in-person or over the phone.*

It's hard saying whether any of these will lead to launch team members, but if you've prepared your vision conversations, more will join the launch team than if you hid in your office depressed.

Let's look at another one.

Output Goal: *I need 200 people to participate in our catalytic event.*

Who wouldn't love to have 200 people at an event! But wanting that doesn't give you any steps on how to accomplish it. In fact, focusing on this goal, especially if it feels overwhelming, might turn people into warm bodies needed to fill a space instead of the beautifully complex people God created them to be. Instead, input goals are actionable and healthy.

Input Goals: *I will prioritize my time to make a plan and set out a timeline for our event. I will seek advice from those who have done this before, invest adequate money and time into marketing, do appropriate research on my local ministry setting, and clearly communicate our plans to the launch team, providing ways for them to volunteer. Then, I will take time at the event to get to know people.*

Output Goal: *I want to start a new church!*

That's great! *But what are you going to do about it?* You can't *wish* a new church into existence. Instead of setting a goal of starting a church, set input-based goals like these.

Input Goal: *I will spend one hour a week thinking, praying, and writing out my vision for this ministry. I will attend appropriate training sessions and read recommended books. I will do one thing each day that helps me get closer to my goal. I will ask people for advice and invite people to come along with me.*

This shift from output to input is hard to make because most denominations and church planting networks measure success from *output*. Leaders want to know how many *baptisms* you had, not how many people you've *invited* to be baptized. Leaders want to know how many people *attended* an event; not how much you *invested* in marketing. When pressure like this is applied, pastors can end up feeling like a failure, and struggle to do anything.

Pressure placed on output goals can often accomplish the opposite of what we intend.

Having expectations placed on pastors that are beyond their control is a major reason for burnout. When we focus on output goals, at best, people tend to freeze up and, at worst, want to quit. Output goals leave people with shallow dreams of what could have been. Input goals give people something to work on and can be easily measured and accomplished.

If you are a supervisor or member of a leadership team, find a way to track your church planter's input goals in place of, or alongside of, their output goals.

Here are a few reasonable input goals for you to keep track of. You might consider making a spreadsheet to track these numbers and use it compare input to output.

How many new people are you meeting each week?

You can't control whether they join the church, get baptized, attend regularly or anything else, but you can control how many you meet. Track how many people you meet each week (input) compared to how many people are at launch team meetings, worship, etc. (output). On average you should plan to meet with 10-15 people each week.

How many community events are you attending each month?

Put every festival, block party, and march on your calendar. Get out there and show up. You can't control who you meet or what you talk about, but you can control whether you show up. Track how many community events you attend (input) and compare it to how many new contacts you make there (output).

Have you planned your Catalytic Event?

Catalytic Events are a great way to meet new people. When you hold your event, track how many new people you're able to meet (input) compared to how many people end up coming to worship as a result (output).

How many people have you emailed and asked to get lunch or coffee this week?

You can't control whether they reply, show up, or respond positively to your invitation, but you *can control* whether you extend it. Track how many people you meet, one-on-one or at gatherings (input), and how many join the launch team (output).

Have you trained those on your launch team about the importance of meeting new people?

You can't make your launch team invite new people, but you do have a say in how much time you commit to your meetings talking about it. The same could be said for growing generous givers and every other part of discipleship. You can't control whether people give, but you can control how you talk about giving. Track how much time you spend with your team on reaching new people (input) with how many stories you hear about them inviting people to events (output).

How often have you posted on social media this week?

You can't control if people see it, like it, comment on it, or share it, but you can control how often you post and what you post about. Learn the best practices of social media and take the time to tell your story. Then track how many social media posts you're doing (input) with how many new people sign up for your email list, express interest, or attend an event (output).

How often have you sent a newsletter to your email list?

You can't control whether people read it, but you can control how often you send one and whether you're following best practices. Add as many people as you can to your newsletter, asking everyone you meet if you can add them, and send it out once, every 1-2 weeks. This allows those who are committed and, on the fence, to stay up-to-date on what you're doing. Track how many newsletters you send (input) to how many people sign up for the launch team, offer to volunteer, give, or any other action steps offered in the newsletter (output).

It might feel like overkill to track all of these metrics each week, but it's worth tracking a few, even if only informally. If you do, you are likely to find a correlation between them. When you don't, take time to properly consider why, but know that it takes far more input to produce results than most people realize.

In many church plant settings, the best ratio of input to output you can expect is 1:3 or 1:4. (In sales, it can be as high as 1:7 or for cold calls, 1:20, but hopefully you're not making random cold calls.) In other words, if your output goal is to have 50 people on your launch team, you will need to set an input goal of meeting with 150 to 200 people. If you've only met with 50 people and you're discouraged you only have 10 people on your launch team, don't be! You're right on track.

This is why planting a church out of an existing church can be easier. If the church has over 200 in worship, one strategic sermon can get you close to your goal. For those starting with less, that will be a lot of new contacts and require you to prioritize your time.

Finally, your launch team will be your biggest asset for inviting people. On average, a committed and energized launch team will bring two people to the Launch service, but it could he higher based on the demographics, training, and culture. Once you get people to attend the first Sunday, the average attendance the following week will drop off substantially, as much as 50-60%. This means if you have 100 people your first Sunday, it's likely you will average 50 your first year. Your launch model and your follow-up processes have a big impact on how much of a drop you can expect to experience. All these factors—and more—can influence the output.

Consider using the **Worship Attendance Calculator** to estimate your worship attendance and launch team goals at **churchplantershandbook.org**.

Setting input goals like these will move a new church forward in ways you could never imagine. Don't get hung up or distracted by what you *hope* will happen. Focus on what you can do to *make* it happen.

Meeting new people is the most important task for a church planter. Make it a priority, and when you can't find as many People of Peace as you want, don't get discouraged. Keep going. Keep searching. Press on. Don't give up and don't lose heart. Shake off the dust and keep trying, and God will take care of the rest.

Church Planter's Toolkit

Go to churchplantershandbook.org to access the following resources related to this chapter:

- **"Meeting New People" Sample Resources:** This includes a few of the resources below as well as a spreadsheet for tracking contacts and a sample response card.
- **"Help us Meeting New People" Handout:** Use this to encourage your launch team to think through who they might invite.
- **Key Components for a One-Pager:** This walks you through the basic requirements for a vision "one-pager."
- **Worship Attendance Calculator:** Use this to set your input and output goals for your church.
- **Tracking People Spreadsheet:** This spreadsheet can be used to track the dozens of conversations you'll be having as you meet new people.

Chapter 7

Building a Launch Team

As Jesus was walking beside the Sea of Galilee, he saw two brothers, Simon called Peter and his brother Andrew. They were casting a net into the lake, for they were fishermen. "Come, follow me," Jesus said, "and I will send you out to fish for people." At once they left their nets and followed him.

Going on from there, he saw two other brothers, James son of Zebedee and his brother John. They were in a boat with their father Zebedee, preparing their nets. Jesus called them, and immediately they left the boat and their father and followed him. (Matthew 4:18-22)

What a beautiful snapshot of Jesus gathering his first disciples. He was building a launch team, even though he wouldn't call it that (and you don't have too either). Whatever you call it, the disciples were the early adopters who came alongside his vision and helped make it a reality.

Thankfully, Jesus didn't teach them to "fish for people" like we do in Ohio, with a pole, fishing line, a lure, and a worm, as if we're meant to lure people into the faith only to snag them on a sharp hook. Some evangelistic techniques feel exactly like this. But these disciples weren't going to catch fish like that. No hooks. No bait-and-switch. No pierced lips. Just a net.

Nets are a really good way of thinking about your launch team.

If you're uncomfortable with fishing metaphors, you can imagine any net you want, whether it's a fishing net, the kind trapeze artists use when they fall, or even a hammock strung between two trees. (A hammock might be my favorite kind of net.) Whatever net you're imagining, nets are designed to catch and hold things for short periods of time. In the same way, a launch team is used to catch or hold future members of the church *before* there is a church.

Jesus's earliest disciples were his launch team. They learned, grew, and formed the foundation of the church before it was fully launched at Pentecost.

In the same way, a well-formed launch team plays a crucial role in laying the groundwork for a new church. In the months leading to your public launch, schedule monthly, weekly, or bi-weekly meetings for your team. Here are some of the key things launch team meetings can help accomplish:

1. It gives you something to invite people to.
2. It gives you a place to share and shape your vision.
3. It provides you a place to train and teach.
4. It gives you time to plan, build teams, and implement your strategy.
5. It helps a growing community remain future-focused.
6. It helps reach new people and new generations.

Let's look at each one in detail.

1. It gives you something to invite people to.

Jesus invited all kinds of people to follow him and when he did, he was inviting them *today*. He wasn't talking about *someday*. Jesus wasn't asking people to stay tuned for Pentecost, when the church would finally start and until then, they'd just have to wait. In fact, he was very serious about the urgency of people following him *today*, saying to one person "No one who puts a hand to the plow and looks back is fit for service in the kingdom of God" (Luke 9:62). Don't pressure people into being on the launch team or act out of a false urgency, but at the same time, when you invite people to be a part of something, it's important you have something for them to be a part of *today*. Often new churches are not ready to start a church until they have enough people, and thus having a launch team, or similar entity, allows a way for someone to move forward with their commitment *before* the church starts.

After all that work of scheduling meetings, going to community events, and meeting with people, you don't want to find yourself with interested people but nothing to invite them to.

There's a traditional church in the suburbs of Columbus that wanted to launch a contemporary service. They followed a process like the one that is laid out in this book. They started by building a launch team, but there was a problem. Their initial launch team was all made up by people who had long attended their traditional church. They were passionate about launching something new, but mostly out of a desire to preserve their current congregation. They also all knew each other. They navigated the internal culture with insider language and already-established relationships. This made recruiting new people to the launch team difficult.

A month before the Launch Sunday, the pastor asked me, "What do you think would be a success for us?" I think he expected me to have some numbers for his Launch Sunday, like "Success is having 100 people on your first Sunday!" No. He needed to realize that real success is *having new people join the launch team.* Finding new people interested in the mission and vision, and willing to serve and lead is always the best sign of success for a new church.

Jesus was successful because he had twelve disciples willing to catch his vision for the world. It wasn't about the size, but the fact they were open to new ideas, committed to the way of Jesus, and willing to go along with Jesus's plan for a new way of practicing their faith—even if they didn't always understand Jesus's vision.

A month later we were chatting, and thanks be to God, there were new people on the launch team! It was exciting. Unlike the established church members, they were there for the mission and the vision and not just institutional preservation. They were eager to invite their friends. On Launch Sunday, it was the new launch team members who invited the most people. This is often the case; it's new people who are the most motivated to make this new church a reality. This is why planting churches works. It's why recruiting and deploying *new* leaders is crucial for launching a church. New leaders will bring new life, vision, and energy to any endeavor and help you get one step closer to sustainability.

Every additional launch team meeting should include new people in attendance, with your current members welcoming them with open arms. In this way, a launch team of five people can grow to 50 as you work to meet new people and train people in the importance of inviting others.

2. It gives you a place to share and shape your vision.

Jesus used parables and personal examples to show his disciples the kind of community he was trying to build. He cast a vision which they would eventually see come to fruition when the church launched in Acts chapter 2. The same is true for the church planter. If you've completed the work of crafting a mission and vision, you already have all the wording, stories, and language needed to create a vision for your new church. When you're with your launch team, take time to reiterate what you hope to see happen.

The key to effective communication of a vision is consistent repetition. Don't be afraid of repeating yourself. People need to hear things more than once for them to sink in.

It's also important to provide space for your launch team to dream and contribute to your mission and vision. A few discussion questions scattered throughout your meetings can help facilitate this.

3. It provides you a place to train and teach.

Jesus shared with his disciples' parables, the sermon on the mount, the sermon on the plain, and countless other incarnational lessons. He showed his disciples how to love the unlovable, how to deal with conflict from staunch religious rulers, how to respect women and hold outcasts in high regard. He ate with people other Rabbis wouldn't eat with and provided for crowds that everyone else was annoyed by. Each of these experiences became lessons for his disciples.

They were learning to be the church.

Launch team meetings are a great way to learn how to be the church, and in a world filled with church hurt, it's also a great place to unlearn unhealthy practices of church too.

Take time in your launch team meetings to teach and train people in the practices that will shape your faith community. This should include, but not be limited to, your expectations for spiritual growth, giving, serving, inviting people, relational excellence, and any other spiritual practices core to your community. Teach on each of these and any others that you hope will shape your faith community.

Here are a few practices worth including:

Give Generously: Remind people of the importance of giving and provide an easy way to give to the church. Ensure you have all of your financial processes up and running before you have launch team meetings, so those who are willing to give can start giving right away. Include a commitment to financially support the church plant as part of a launch team covenant. The only way to grow generous givers is to include it in every part of the discipleship process. Like everything else, you're not guilt-tripping, shaming, or talking people into giving. Instead, share the reasons why giving is not only important for the church but for the person who gives. Remind people of the transformation that happens in our hearts when we are generous and the impact they will be able to have as a church when everyone contributes what they can.

> Growing Generous Givers
>
> In the midst of the launch season, there is a lot to think about, cover, and accomplish. It's easy to forget to mention the importance of giving. Here's why you can't leave this out. People tend not to give right away. They need time to think and pray and process. People will often give months after their first invitation to give. The longer you put off talking about the importance of giving, the longer it will take for your launch team to start making that commitment.

Serve Regularly: The only way to successfully launch a new church is to move new people into places of service quickly. While you'll need to develop your own strategy for recruiting volunteers, here's a simple process to get started:

1. **Communicate/Announce:** Teach/preach the importance of serving and clearly communicate all the unique places people can serve and why those roles are important to the mission. In many ways, teaching on the importance of serving and announcing places where you need volunteers will help prepare the soil. Most people won't sign up to serve from this alone, but it will help open them up to the idea.
2. **Discern**: Provide a way for people to reflect on and evaluate their unique gifts, talents, and strengths. Celebrate the diversity of your community and remind people that each person has gifts that are unique and needed by God to accomplish your mission. This could be done through a formal assessment (spiritual gifts inventory, personality assessment, etc.), through time for reflection (reflection guide, questions, etc.), and teaching/preaching (workshops and teachings on spiritual gifts or the importance of the diversity).
3. **Ask**: In the end, most people will serve because you ask them. The work done to preach, teach, announce, and provide ways to discern are great for preparing people and inviting them to consider the possibility of serving, but for most, the only way to translate that from a place of consideration to commitment is when you or another leader personally asks them. Don't rely on announcements or mass emails to get volunteers. Find a way to go up to someone and ask. Remember, whenever you ask someone for anything, it's ok for them to say no. Remind yourself that, so that you don't take advantage of the unequal power dynamics between religious leaders and those we serve.

Radical Hospitality: A new church must excel at welcoming new people, intentionally investing in friendly and welcoming practices. The whole point of launching a new church is to connect with new people, but without proper training in culturally relevant hospitality practices, a new church can fall short of being a welcoming place.

Most churches think they were friendly, but sadly, very few churches thrive at hospitality. Seeing yourself as friendly or allowing hospitality to happen "naturally" or "informally" will not produce the results you want. Hospitality takes intentional, thoughtful processes and training. It doesn't happen simply because you value it as an idea or theological construct. It happens because you *practice* it. Take time to identify and train your launch team on what hospitality looks like in your setting. This might include things like trained greeters, visitor gifts, follow-up processes, connect cards, avoiding religious jargon, visitor events, and more.

Risk-taking Mission: Jesus consistently forces his disciples to interact with and process the important work of justice and mercy. Whether it be the woman caught in adultery, the woman at the well, the blind, the demon-possessed, or anyone else who was discarded or ignored, Jesus loved those often tossed aside, bringing his disciples along and helping them learn the importance of loving the least of these (Matthew 9:10-13, Matthew 25). Take time, before you even become a church, to invest in mission, service, and cross-cultural experiences. Do it with integrity, from a sincere place, with curiosity and humility, and help your launch team process these experiences through robust theological reflections.

Reclaiming Evangelism: A new church, no matter what kind it is, will only be as effective as its ability to connect with new people. Teaching your launch team the importance of meeting new people, the power of an invitation, and creative ways to reclaim evangelism is essential. Here are a few ideas we've found helpful in a variety of church plant models:

- **Ask people to share their faith story.** This helps people get comfortable talking about their faith, moving their faith from an experience or idea to something they can articulate.
- **Allow people to speak into your worship and outreach events.** People are far more likely to invite someone to something if they are excited about it and feel ownership in it.
- **Provide diverse ways to invite people.** For example, you could ask some people to go door-to-door to hang door hangers. Others might be willing to stand at a table at a local festival to

promote your church. Provide various levels of engagement, respecting people's boundaries and limitations.

- Visit the chapters on **Meeting New People** and **Reclaiming Evangelism** for additional ideas you can use with your launch team.

There are likely other essential practices that make sense for your church model. For example, Allyssa built a launch team of leaders starting their own faith communities and mission endeavors, so learning how to start something from scratch and invite people into it, was essential for her team. On the other hand, if you're trying to start a church for people across the political spectrum to be in community together, you should include training on how to have difficult conversations. If you hope to be multi-ethnic, or diverse, do the work to understand implicit bias, systemic racism, etc. Whatever your vision, provide training to make it a reality for your launch team members.

4. It gives you time to plan, build teams, and implement your strategy.

Jesus used his time with his disciples to create systems and teams. Peter was put in charge, John and James were given leadership opportunities, and they even had a treasurer. The fact that the treasurer didn't work out should be an encouragement to anyone who put someone in leadership only to realize they were the wrong fit.

A launch team is the place to start recruiting leaders, building teams, and preparing what you need to make the church a reality.

Here are a few things to consider as you implement your strategy:

- **Ministry Action Plan:** Go back and revisit your MAP and walk through the relevant parts with your launch team and key leaders so they can understand the timeline, big picture, and strategy.
- **Ministry Teams:** What ministry teams do you need to launch your church? Form these during the launch phase, spotlight these teams during the meeting, and use some of your launch team meetings for your teams to collaborate.

- **Timeline:** Take time to lay out the timeline, helping people see where you're headed. People will always get more excited about something when they know there's a clear plan.

Take time in your launch team meetings to walk through the overarching plan so that as many people as possible can understand and join the process.

5. It helps a growing community remain future-focused.

A year ago, Allyssa started brainstorming a new church called Open Church. She dreamed of a network of fresh expressions, faith communities, and mission ventures that engaged in ministry through intentional practices and a shared vision. She started with an essential question: Could we launch a new church that wasn't centered on a Sunday morning experience? Since launching, she has dozens of fresh expressions and missional communities. For example, on Wednesday night there's a recovery community on the westside of Columbus, on Sundays is a gathering at a house church, and next month, there's a small group that is planning to meet in a local pub to discuss big questions about their faith. There's a college ministry at Ohio State University, street outreach in Linden, and a non-alcoholic drink service that raises money for recovery efforts. This is what Open Church ended up becoming, but it's not how it started.

At the beginning, she was busy gathering a launch team like we had before—a group of interested people. She invited them into our living room on a weekly basis for worship and discipleship. After a couple of months, she wasn't sure how to take that launch team and translate it into her vision of a network of microchurches. Those attending her weekly house church were happy with the experience. They weren't looking for anything else. They pushed back against the invitations and vision that there might be a collective of dozens of these fresh expressions all over the city. In short, this gathering in our home wasn't a launch team because they weren't interested in launching what's next. They were a faith community and there's nothing wrong with a faith community—it's ultimately what we're trying to start—but if a launch team becomes a church before it's ready, it will get stuck there forever.

In the end, Allyssa had to stop thinking of her house church as a launch team. After some brainstorming, she decided to stop gathering a community in our home and instead focused on equipping leaders to gather their own communities.

She set a goal of having five faith communities or missional endeavors by the fall at her launch. And instead of a typical Launch Day that results in weekly services, she held a commissioning service for these leaders.

As she met people and shared the vision, she invited them into an intentional leadership training, which she hosted in our home again, but this time with a different purpose. They weren't gathering to be the church; they were gathering to learn how to launch one.

Of the eight who attended, five went on to launch a new faith community with Open Church and two others decided to merge their already-established faith communities into the Open Church Network. By fall, she brought seven leaders up front on her Launch Day commissioning service, where they introduced themselves, shared in a commissioning liturgy and were prayed over by our District Superintendent.

She had to redirect her energy to recruiting and training the leaders who would start those faith expressions and missional endeavors instead of pastoring those who were happy with the status quo. It was a difficult pivot to make, but if your launch team becomes comfortable, you'll have to do the same.

A launch team must remain forward-thinking, invested in what was next, and not comfortable keeping things as they are. Launch teams that are comfortable with the status quo won't launch anything.

6. It helps reach new people & new generations.

Seven years ago, a group of 25 people gathered in a small church fellowship hall for our first launch team meeting of Central City Church. A friend led us in a few songs, and then Allyssa and I shared our vision for a new church.

After I was done, we broke into small groups and encouraged people to start dreaming about the kind of church we might become.

It's a beautiful memory. Recently, I went back and looked at the photos from that first launch team meeting and noticed something that broke my heart. I saw only one person in those photos who is still a part of our church.

I was warned this might be the case. Most of the people who help you launch will not be at your church five years later.

In some ways, we even see this in the example of Jesus. In the four Gospels, years before Paul would ever become a follower of Jesus, there were twelve disciples. Jesus invested in these twelve disciples, and they were the leaders who helped launch Christianity into the world. Yet, a quick survey of the New Testament and you will find that the leaders of note change rather quickly. It's Paul, Timothy, Barnabas, Lydia, and hundreds of others who carry the good news throughout the Roman Empire.

Sure, Peter, James and a few others get some mentions, but in general, the stories of the early church don't center around the twelve disciples.

Wouldn't it have been easier for Jesus to *start* with Paul and skip over the twelve disciples? No. Because God knows, what we often forget. Life is filled with seasons, and in those seasons, everyone has a role to play. When it's your turn, you need to jump in and give it your all and then move forward without disdain when God brings new people to carry the message forward.

How could anyone be upset when God brings new people to carry the message? Wasn't that the whole point? You're doing this to give new people a chance to *become* the body of Christ. You can't be sad or discouraged by that, and it certainly shouldn't make anyone feel insecure.

It needs to be celebrated.

God will send you people to serve on the launch team, and that might be all they do. That's ok. They are like "scaffolding"—essential, but never permanent. God will provide what you need to build the church, but once it's built, those people might move on.

United Methodist pastors commit to itinerancy. This means that they recognize that their time at a church is limited and that they should never build a church around their individual personalities. They need to be willing to go where God sends them. What United Methodists often fail to recognize is that lay leadership can also be itinerant. The leaders who carried a church in one season might not be the leaders God has for the next. As much as God calls pastors to refrain from building a church around their personality, God is calling lay leaders to do the same. Far too many small, generational churches are built around the personality of a few strong-willed individuals.

Six years after launching, we have no one in leadership from our launch team, but we have quite a few people in leadership who attended the first Sunday—and wasn't that the point?

A launch team will help you start a church that provides new places for new people.

What a Launch Team *Isn't*

- **A board or decision-making body.** The season surrounding a new church isn't a good time to start a board or leadership team. If you are required to have one, there should be an intentional process for adding board members that includes a job description, application, and interview. If you have a board, be sure that your launch team isn't it. A careful survey of the Gospels shows us why the twelve disciples were only made leaders in the church *after* the resurrection. They needed time to understand Jesus's vision for church. A launch team isn't ready to make significant decisions. It's created to hold a community of people growing together until the church launches. A church planter still needs accountability during this season, but that should come from a parent church, district, network, coach, or advisory team. Let the launch team serve as a net that catches anyone interested in your new church.
- **A closed group of church people who all know each other.** If a launch team is filled with friends and church people, it will be hard for new people to join. The focus must be on connecting with new people. Jesus didn't recruit established religious leaders

or prominent members of the synagogue for a reason. Starting with fishermen and tax collectors—those new to the faith or on the fringes—ensured Jesus was able to connect with others like them. Don't look for overly qualified or experienced people. Instead, look for people who are excited about the vision, willing to learn, and invite. Established church people have long exhausted their network of friends. All their friends either already attend church or have already been invited. When we reach new people, we're also connecting with a brand-new circle of influence.

- **A room of warm bodies**. A launch team can't be a room full of people uninterested in the church plant. You're looking for People of Peace who are passionate about trying something new. If you fill the launch team with people who are there entirely out of obligation, institutional preservation, or skepticism, you'll find your team becomes more of an anchor holding everything back than a spring that could launch it forward.
- **A permanent group.** The launch team is temporary. While it's a high commitment, the commitment doesn't have to be forever, which makes it all the easier for inviting anyone and everyone to it. When forming a more intentional, long-term team of leaders and volunteers, you'll want to take time to screen and interview people more than you would for a launch team.

Launch teams are for anyone interested in starting something new.

Reflection

- Will you build a launch team? If so, what will it look like given your vision for church? What will you call it?
- What is your church's rule of life? What practices are you asking your church members and leaders to engage in on a regular basis? How will you share this with your team that is helping you start?
- Name one key practice that you need to train your launch team that wasn't mentioned above.
- How will you invite your launch team or similar entity to give to the church?

- What processes do you have in place for new people to get involved and build relationships?
- How will you keep your launch team future-oriented?

Church Planter's Toolkit

Go to churchplantershandbook.org to access the following resources related to this chapter:

- **Custom Church Timeline & Checklists:** Revisit this so you can share with your team your overall strategy.
- **Launch Team Covenant:** This sample covenant can be edited and used to help potential launch team members prayerfully consider what it means to serve on the launch team.
- **"Help us Meet New People" Handout:** Use this to get your team thinking about who they might invite to be a part of this new church.
- **Sharing Your Faith Story:** Use this to get your launch team more comfortable articulating what they believe.

To access the Church Planter's Toolkit at churchplantershandbook.org,enter this passcode: PLANT!TOOLS

Chapter 8

Recruiting Leaders

Church plants take an immense amount of initiative. You have to start everything from scratch—there is no committee to rely on until you form it, no staff to work with until you hire them, no money to spend until you raise it. You want to get a full-time salary? You have to form the budget and find the funds. You want to have worship? You have to find the location and you need to recruit a good worship leader. You want to have children's ministry? Find the staff and volunteers, write the safe sanctuary policy, and raise the money to pay for it. The task set before a church planter is monumental and can at times feel overwhelming.

The worst thing you can do is try to do all of this by yourself. Your greatest tool is to recruit, train, and deploy high-impact volunteers and leaders to carry the burden. Here's how you do it in a church plant:

1. Identify essential roles.
2. Fundraise as needed.
3. Develop staff processes.
4. Recruit the staff you need.
5. Provide onboarding and mentoring.
6. Schedule regular feedback and accountability.
7. Provide benefits that help balance the cost of serving in the church.

1. Identify Essential Roles

Church planting is all about *people building*. We gather people, invest in leaders, and build systems, often from scratch.

It's embarrassing to admit, but when we launched, we didn't have a children's ministry. We had space for kids. We had a few tables and chairs. We had a nursery, set up next to the bar in the theater we rented. We had invested thousands of dollars for the children's space to be designed by Church in the Box and even had a team to help set up the space. We had summer interns who we paid to take care of the nursery, but no children's ministry. On our grand opening, we had a few volunteers pass out coloring pages, which Allyssa printed off the night before.

We didn't have a children's ministry because we didn't have a leader to provide vision, strategy, and care for our families. The same was true for worship—we had a few willing volunteers but no leader. Starting a church that centered on the Sunday experience and geared towards young families *without* an experienced person in worship or children's ministry cost us.

We launched with 150 and quickly shrunk to 50. The few families who stayed did so for the mission, not the amenities (and there's good in that too).

As you consider your vision and hopes for your new church, remember that you will only be able to accomplish what you have leaders to initiate.

What are the core elements of your vision, and do you have trusted leaders to oversee them?

When pastors step into established churches, there are clear roles and often existing staff. In a church plant, not only are there often no other staff, but there are no existing roles. You have to take time to hold up your strategy to the light and identify the roles you need to make it a reality.

Whether they are paid or unpaid doesn't matter as much as whether they are a trusted, identified leader in that area capable of casting vision and managing details. Depending on how important the leadership role is, determines how much you need to invest into it. If gathering people for worship is your primary tool for bringing people together, then having a good worship leader is very important. If you're launching a network of fresh expressions or microchurches, then finding the leaders to lead those micro communities is essential. The more important the role, the more energy, time and money you will need to invest in finding the right leaders and preparing them to lead well.

2. Fundraise as Needed

Staffing is often one of the largest expenses in a church—the more paid roles you hope to have, the more funding you will require. When deciding whether to have a role be paid or unpaid, take a few things into consideration. **1. How essential is the role?** If you can live without the role for a few weeks, you might be able to put off hiring something. **2. How much time does the role take?** According to the US Bureau of Labor Statistics in 2022, around 4.7 million people volunteer on average 1.56 to 2.23 hours in a day, depending on the type of volunteer work,[1] and according to Network for Good, most people only volunteer on average 3.5 hours a week.[2] This is the average, so it's possible that depending on life stage, personal needs, and capacity, some volunteers can put in a lot more hours than the average, especially for short seasons, like a launch season. But in general, if the role requires more time than an average person can do in a week while also working full-time, then you'll need to either split the role up or pay someone. It's unhealthy to expect volunteers to work full-time and then put in an unhealthy number of volunteer hours. **3. Do you have someone in your community who can fill the role as a volunteer?** If you have someone there with gifts and talents that line up with your needs, then find a way to help them lean into this gifting, even if it means accommodating their limited time. In the end, we're the body of Christ, and your job is to equip and empower people to use their gifts. If you don't, and it's an essential role, you might need to hire from the outside.

Once you've laid out your essential roles and considered which would be paid and unpaid, finalize your budget. Weigh the church's needs against your ability to fundraise and adjust.

A church plant's budget should include diverse funding sources. According to Barna's book *Church Startups and Money*[3] the percentage of churches that felt they had more than sufficient funding, received funding from the following sources:

- Another church other than parent church
- Tithes and offerings
- Individuals who do not attend the church
- Church planting grant
- Planter's personal network or family members
- Parent church
- Non-church planting grant

Your fundraising strategy needs to take place before, during, and after your launch season, pulling from as many different sources of income as you can. Over the first few years as a new church, the goal is to grow in attendance and giving so that the majority of these sources can be replaced by your offering or other long-term funding opportunities. When socio-economic barriers keep this from happening, long-term support and creative fundraising needs to be secured and nurtured throughout the life of the church.

Here are the four most important lessons in church planting fundraising:

1. **Church planting costs money.** The more you strategically invest into the launch, the better it will go. Grassroots, organic church planting models are wonderful, and lean into affordable options as best you can. But statistically, the more you invest the more likely it will become sustainable long-term.
2. **It's no one else's responsibility to make sure that you have enough funding.** This is the primary job of the church planter—there is no guarantee that your launch team, conference, or sending church is going to take on this responsibility, until you teach them how. Entitlement or feeling like there's a mysterious source of income out there that someone is withholding from your church plant will do more to hurt your fundraising efforts than anything else. No one, including your conference, is obligated to fund your church plant. Instead operate from the assumption that people will want to fund it *once* they hear the vision, and you ask them to contrib-

ute. "Ask and it will be given" if you ask from a place of vision and humility.

3. **People enjoy being generous.** When was the last time someone asked for a refund on a donation? They don't. When people give, they do it because they want to. It's life-giving, and beautiful. The only hard part of giving is thinking about it ahead of time. Once you've released the funds, endorphins and joy are released. It's great and transforming! Don't feel bad about asking for financial support. Keep your vision strategic, your ask specific, and your donation processing simple and you'll see people step up to the challenge.
4. **Practice what you preach.** Give 10% of your income to the church plant and invite your launch team to do the same. Never ask people to do to something you're unwilling to do yourself.

Once you've identified your essential roles and implemented your fundraising strategy, it's time to lay out your staff processes.

3. Develop Staff Processes

Having a process for hiring and recruiting leaders is essential not only to ensuring ethical practices but also to the overall health of your new church.

Here are some of the basic steps you need to implement for every leadership position, paid or unpaid. This includes board members, staff, or anyone else who is involved in leading people, spending money, or setting policy.

- **Job Description:** You can't hold someone accountable to something they are unaware of. This is why job descriptions are essential. Job descriptions provide clear, written descriptions of what's expected, and provide a launching point for ongoing conversation and accountability.
- **Interview**: One of the easiest mistakes a church plant can make is to give friends and advocates top leadership positions without walking candidates through an equitable process of mutual discernment. Take time to interview people, especially when you're desperate to fill the role, or there's only one candidate, or

you're hoping to fill the role with a friend. The worst thing you can do in a church plant is put the wrong person into a position of influence simply because they are willing, or you like them. Make sure your interviews include more than the lead pastor or supervisor so multiple perspectives can speak to the quality of the candidate. It's easy to skip over job descriptions and interviews for unpaid staff. It's easy to be so worried about filling the role and feel bad about making someone do it as a volunteer, that you don't want to add anything else to their plate. *Why would I make them do an interview if they barely want to serve as it is?* Here's why. If a volunteer is willing to serve, but unwilling to complete an application or be interviewed, they aren't actually willing to serve. By having this step, you automatically weed out anyone doing it for the wrong reasons.

- **Offer**: Make the offer, and pray they accept it—but be sure it's the offer you want to make. Out of desperation, it's tempting to bring people onto staff that you might later regret. Fear of not having enough, or the overarching scarcity mindset that is pervasive in a new church start, can trick us into offering jobs to the wrong people. Sometimes you must make it work with the people you have, but in many situations it's better to go without a staff member than to hire the wrong one. The best way to decide which way to go is to have a group of caring and committed people around you to help you make these hard decisions. The offer should include clarity around pay, start dates, job description, and anything else needed for them to make their decision.
- **Organizational Chart:** Having a simple chart that shows who reports to whom is an easy way to keep everyone on the same page. Include this in your staff orientation and future board manual. Remember, clear is kind. You might need to explain this organizational chart to your congregation as well. In small, established churches it's common for staff to "work for the church." In other words, a church administrator or secretary is the secretary for the entire church. Similar views can be held about the pastor—the pastor works for us. This is unhealthy

> and can make showing up to work unbearable. A clear organizational chart, that is enforced and communicated, helps everyone practice healthy boundaries. In the United Methodist Church, the pastor reports to their District Superintendent and Bishop, and is appointed to their church to serve in partnership with a board which they also serve as a member. The board oversees the congregation, not the pastor. The staff, then, should report directly to the pastor or their designee. All of this can be clearly communicated in a simple organizational chart. There are a few examples of what this could look like in the *Church Planter's Toolkit.*

4. Recruit the Staff You Need

Our church needed a new worship leader.

We had heard from a conference staff member of a worship leader who might be interested in the position. We found out that he owned a brewery in the northern part of Columbus, and that he was hanging out at the brewery that night. Allyssa and I strapped Finn into the car seat and drove 30 minutes to the brewery, where our friend introduced us. We talked to him about our church and told him about our needs. A week later we got lunch, and a few weeks after that, Ryan Wilkins became our worship leader. Later, when he moved on from our church, he went and led worship for one of Allyssa's new churches, and his friend, Dan, who had played at our church with Ryan, applied for the open position. Dan has been our worship leader ever since, leading our community through a merger and working hard to create collaboration with the traditional musicians our church merged with. We have had a great worship leader for the last 5 years because Allyssa and I decided to hop in the car and drive to a brewery to meet someone and they were nice enough to say "yes."

In a church planet, staff are recruited more often than they are hired. Yes, once you recruit them, they need to go through the proper processes as mentioned above, but often people won't apply unless they are asked. Finding high-impact staff is the same as finding launch team members: you have to networking, make introductions, leverage your network, ask around, and take time getting to know as many people as possible.

While every position is different, here are some of the qualities to look for in potential leaders to recruit:

1. **They have diverse perspectives and gifts.** A more diverse team fosters creativity and innovation, and better reflects the communities served by your church. Be open to new ideas and different perspectives and invite those with different experiences into your inner circle. Diversity is a strength because you can't do everything by yourself. You need people who are good at the stuff you struggle with and see things you don't notice. A healthy leader will be aware of their own weaknesses and celebrate people who show strengths in that area. Paul says it well in his letter to the Corinthians: The church is like a body, and the body is made up of many parts. It would be silly for an eye to try and be an ear, or a nose to try and be the feet. Instead, be on the lookout for the parts of the body you're missing, and when you see someone excel in an area where there is a need, encourage it.
2. **They are gifted in bringing people together.** The main goal of a church plant is to gather people. A church plant needs leaders who are gifted in hospitality, event planning, and including those on the margins. You need as many leaders as you can who are gifted in gathering people. Every staff member, from administration to children's ministry, should have gifts in hospitality.
3. **They are generous.** Generosity isn't coerced, it's inspired. The more generous you and your leaders are, the more likely others will be inspired to be generous. Practice generosity in all areas of your church and watch your community follow your example.
4. **They know how to build teams.** Leaders aren't there to only accomplish tasks. Good leaders are going to know how to recruit, train, and deploy volunteers. By definition, a leader is someone who leads other people. In this case, you need leaders who are investing in other people and providing ways for them to accomplish the mission of the church.

5. **They have a vision for their ministry area and can communicate it to others.** Your leaders will speak to groups of people you will never be given access to. It's important they can articulate the vision for the church and their ministry area in relevant and contextual ways.
6. **They are able to start things from scratch, or the willingness to learn.** Leading in a church plant is different from an established church. In a church plant, you're building everything from scratch. You're looking for leaders who are willing to engage in this unique kind of work.
7. **They are a self-starter, self-motivated.** You're not looking for someone who just wants to collect a paycheck or add a title to their resume. You're looking for people who will put in the effort to build something from scratch, and often a church plant operates without offices or a physical location. It's important to have leaders who can be creative in how they accomplish their tasks. Look for these people. You might even pause during a launch team meeting or worship service and look for the people who are picking up the trash, or intentionally walking up to chat with a visitor, or helping set up or tear down—without being asked. They are the leaders you need to invest in.
8. **They can be strategic in how to use resources and implement the budget in their ministry area.** A church plant will need to do a lot with a little. Strategic leaders will be able to be thoughtful and clever in how they manage their ministry's budget and flexible when resources run low.

5. Provide Onboarding & Mentorship

Whether it's paid or unpaid staff, take time to develop an orientation that lays out clear expectations, a job description, church values, administrative requirements, and policy.

You can also assign a mentor from within your organization to guide the new leader during the initial months. For example, it's common for volunteers to shadow a ministry area before serving in it, and the same principle can be applied to all levels of leadership.

Mentoring, internship, and apprenticeship are great tools for raising up new leaders. Mentoring leaders ensures that new leaders receive ongoing support, feedback, and insights that help them navigate challenges and make informed decisions. At the start of the new church, the church planter might be the only mentor. If you're able to invest in leaders well, this should grow naturally in such a way that those you have invested in are now able to invest in others.

When looking for leaders, you're looking for people who are going to have a good working relationship with you. They respect you, and more importantly, they are interested in learning from you, meeting with you, and being mentored by you. Try to avoid people who only want to be paid to do the job, and are not interested in anything else as they are often difficult to get a meeting with and unwilling to incorporate feedback into their work.

Building something from scratch is too important to be left to organizational silos. The reality is that many people experience organizational silos in other work environments and are not used to collaboration, mutual respect, or deep listening that is needed in a start-up. In start-ups, roles often blend, and everyone must work together to make it a success. It takes time for those who are willing to learn a new work culture to adapt. If it's a matter of time, give them the time they need. But if they show no signs of being interested in adapting to this new kind of work culture, they might end up being more of a distraction than an asset.

6. Provide Regular Feedback & Accountability

Offer learning opportunities for new leaders at your launch team meetings, vision gatherings, and other professional development events. Anytime you gather potential leaders together, take time to teach on basic values and rhythms that are meant to shape your community. When problems arise, conflict ensues, or confusion begins to brew, take time to debrief, treating each hard lesson as a training opportunity for your leaders.

Leaders will learn more from how you handle conflict than they will ever learn in a workshop.

Whatever you do, invest in your leaders. An ill-equipped employee in an established organization can go unnoticed for years. A start-up doesn't have this luxury. An ill-equipped employee, especially in a top leadership position, can be the end to a fragile church plant.

Working in a church plant requires different skills than other places of work. Leaders have to be able to iterate, adapt, experiment, and persevere. It takes hustle to make it work. They don't have to be good at starting things if they are willing to learn and be coached, but these expectations need to be clear, and they have to be open to learning a new way to work.

Having said that, it's also possible that the church planter needs to adjust their expectations as well. It's not uncommon for church planters to look at underperforming staff who came highly recommended and say, "I just want you to do your job!" A church planter with innate drive and intuition can't always understand someone who is used to a traditional place of employment. They might be doing the job the only way they know how and will need clear and effective communication and mentoring to reach the standards you are looking for. This is why having a regular feedback loop and reviews are important.

Recently we had our staff develop questions they felt would be useful to answer as part of their annual review. We've found these questions are both life-giving and help keep both the staff and their supervisors accountable to healthy leadership practices. Since the staff came up with them, they tend to engage with the questions with sincerity and authenticity. You can use these or even better, ask your staff for the questions they'd want to be asked.

- **Job Performance**: Look over your job description. How does the work you are doing line up with your job description?
- **Self-care:** What are you doing to take care of yourself? How are your boundaries with the people you are serving?
- **Challenges:** What's your biggest challenge this season?
- **Passion:** What are you most excited about?
- **Gifts:** How are your gifts being used in your job? Are there gifts that you have that aren't being used? Are there things that are killing your soul that are not a part of your gifting?

It's possible (and likely) for mission-driven leaders to give above and beyond what is expected, and if you're not careful, a pastor can easily take advantage of this. Work hard to ensure your leaders don't get burnt out and develop healthy boundaries and practices. Accountability isn't just making sure a leader is doing enough but also making sure they aren't doing too much.

7. Provide Benefits That Help Balance the Cost of Serving in a Church

Churches can't afford to pay people grandiose wages, especially in church plants. Many staff at church work part-time or as volunteers. At the same time, ministry is hard. It has an emotional and spiritual toll on leaders. If a pastor wants to keep effective leaders healthy, they must invest in their staff's well-being. When pastors are intentionally generous to their staff, they are inspired to be generous in return. *Remember, generosity isn't coerced, it's inspired. Practice generosity in all areas of your church.*

Here are a few benefits you can offer that don't cost you very much but go a long way to helping staff maintain healthy boundaries and can help retain high-impact leaders:

> **Time Off:** Give people 3-4 weeks of vacation and additional sick leave. Giving people time off costs you nothing but is an amazing benefit. Since the goal in staff is for them to build teams, this also helps motivate them to have the volunteers needed to cover for them. Encouraging people to take time off while expecting them to build the teams to cover when they are gone is a win-win. Work hard to not make them feel guilty about using their time off. This will go a long way to keeping your staff happy and healthy. Also, when you build a culture that encourages people to take time off, staff will encourage each other to get away, often helping cover for each other when needed. All of this helps build a church culture that values rest and collaboration.
>
> **Efficient Processes**: Work to ensure the culture and processes are life-giving wherever possible. In every way you can, make it easier for your staff to do their job, not harder. This can be done in many different little ways. Find out where your staff are spending

their time doing things that frustrate them, and come up with creative, automated ways to make things easier. For example, provide credit cards to staff so they can buy what they need without having to be reimbursed. Imagine being paid part-time and expected to pay for all of your ministry expenses from your own bank account, only to wait a week or two to be reimbursed? No thanks. By giving a staff member a credit card, not only does it make their job 100 times easier, but they will also feel empowered and trusted. You can also set up direct deposit for staff payroll instead of cutting paper checks. Imagine working hard all week, only to have to track down your paycheck, deposit it manually, and wait for it to clear before paying bills. By using direct deposit, you not only make payroll seamless and reliable, but you also show staff that you respect their time and financial stability. Other examples include:

- Use a shared calendar for scheduling instead of relying on scattered emails and texts.
- Use a scheduling app for volunteers so things can be done far in advance, and automatic reminders are sent out without having to remember. Anytime you can take advantage of technology to automatically schedule, remind, or otherwise organize your volunteers, you're going to save your staff loads of wasted time.
- Store important files in a cloud-based system to avoid having to track down the right paperwork.

Due to unhealthy cultures and power dynamics, it's often common in an organization hierarchy for those at the top to make things more difficult for those lower on the rungs. There's this strange tendency for those in authority to think that if we make our staff's jobs easier, we're not getting what we paid for. Fight against this tendency with everything you have (Matthew 20:25). Make life easier for those volunteering or working for the church. Making work unnecessarily tedious is a great way to attract ineffective leaders.

Equitable Pay: Don't pay minimum wage, or anything close to it. Start out at a living wage, regardless of position or job. If you can pay more, do it. Be transparent about your church finances, offering raises when you can, expanding positions when you're able, and ensure that the lead pastor isn't making an unreasonable amount of money compared to those they serve. There are churches where the senior pastor makes ten times as much as the other staff. This level of disproportionate pay is unfair and inequitable, and it can create a very real separation between the pastor and the people they are leading.

Value Gifts, Not Hours: Pay people a salary, even if they are part-time. High-impact leaders can do more in an hour than low-impact leaders can do in a day. Paying high-impact leaders hourly fails to appreciate what they bring to the table. When you pay part-time staff a salary, leaders know that the church appreciates what they can accomplish, not just the hours they worked. It also makes payroll easier, thus saving administrative time as well. They might need to track hours, as it does provide necessary legal protections to both the staff and the church. But have them track hours to ensure they aren't working too much as well.

Don't measure the effectiveness of a staff person based on the number of hours they work, but the level of work they accomplish. Are they building teams, leading events, and accomplishing the tasks laid out in the job description? If they are doing what is needed, and contributing to the healthy culture of the church, while also not working more than is expected, then they are succeeding. This shift in attitude is a small, but a valuable benefit to part-time employees. For high-performing part-time staff, they love the flexibility to work when they need, without set office hours or required hours each week. This kind of flexibility allows high-performing staff control over their schedule. It costs nothing but is often experienced as an added benefit. Having said that, adjust this model as needed. For those who are neurodiverse or tempted to work overtime, they might find the structure of set hours helpful. Do what's most helpful by listening sincerely to your part-time staff needs.

Technology: Provide email addresses for paid and unpaid staff that use the domain of your church, and provide essential staff with laptops, iPads, etc. This technology belongs to the church and can be passed down to new staff as people move on, but providing these technology resources is an overall affordable way to increase your staff's experience of work. Plan on spending around $800-1000 per staff (in 2025 dollars). While that might sound like a lot, it is amazing what people can do when they have the proper technology. (You might also consider allowing your staff to purchase their laptops from the church at a market-rate when they leave their position—just another benefit that leaves people excited about being a part of your church.)

Encouragement. Be encouraging and share gratitude. It's free, and it makes all the difference. Make a point to tell our paid and unpaid staff how grateful you are for them as often as you can. It's sad, but many church volunteers have gone years without being thanked. Being grateful for paid and unpaid leaders (and encouraging your leaders to be grateful and encouraging to their volunteers) is free. It doesn't cost you anything. Give it away like it. It will make all the difference, especially in the high stakes work of church planting.

Little things like this can go a long way to preventing burnout. Ensure your staff is well taken care of, and it will pay dividends for years. Well-supported, properly equipped, and encouraged part-time employees can do more with their half-time than many full-time employees can in unsupported environments.

Leadership Makes the Difference

Be encouraged. God will send you the leaders you need.

Having the right leaders in place to execute the mission is essential to building a healthy church. Finding people to invest in, build trust with, and deploy into ministry is how a church plant goes from an idea to a fully-functioning, sustainable ministry.

It's one thing to gather a group of random people and brainstorm what a church could look like. It's something else entirely to take that random group, find the leaders amongst them, and move them into places needed to execute the mission God has given you. But you can't do it without this. Just like Moses learned the hard way (Exodus 18:24-27), it seems most of us still have to learn the hard way. When you try to do it all yourselves, you will become overwhelmed and fail to accomplish your goals.

Jesus didn't start by launching a church—that came later. He started with investing in a small group of people.

A new church doesn't start with weekly worship services or local missions. It starts by recruiting, equipping, and deploying leaders.

Reflection

- What experience do you have in recruiting volunteer leaders or hiring staff?
- Considering your vision for the church, what are 3-5 essential leaders needed before you launch?
- What are your strengths and what are your weaknesses? Do you find it easy to celebrate those who excel in the areas you struggle? Why or why not?
- When looking for a leader, what are the most important qualities you look for?

Church Planter's Toolkit

Go to churchplantershandbook.org to access the following resources related to this chapter:

- **Sample Job Descriptions:** Use this tool to start creating effective leadership job descriptions.
- **Church Organizational Charts:** Use these as an example of what an effective organizational chart can look like, at various seasons in the church plant's life.
- **Sample Staff Policy:** Get a head start on creating policies with this editable staff policy.

Chapter 9

Reclaiming Evangelism

A few years ago, I preached a series on evangelism. I was proud of this sermon series. We talked about what the gospel means, how to discuss our faith with people who don't share the same beliefs, and how to reclaim evangelism from the toxic, overbearing, trigger-producing, harmful proselyte version of evangelism some of us were raised in. The kind of aggressive evangelism that starts with going up to a stranger and asking them "If you died today, do you know if you would go to heaven?"

Have you ever done this?

If not, consider yourself lucky.

This series pushed back against this kind of thinking and approach. It offered a healthier way, but for some, that didn't matter. Just seeing the series title of "Evangelism" was too much.

They weren't interested. I remember one person in particular. We announced the series the week before it kicked off. When she saw it was about evangelism, she was out. She told me she was going to take a break from church. She didn't want to be a part of a church that *talked* about evangelism.

You see, the pressure and expectation and toxic ways people have done evangelism didn't line up with what she believed, so she didn't want to be a part of a church that even discussed such things.

It was a trigger.

I was sad though. What we talked about was far more inclusive and welcoming than what she was worried about.

This isn't the only time this has happened.

We had a guest preacher do a sermon on the importance of sharing their faith. Afterward, one of our members decided to take a break from church. It was too much.

There's no shame in having triggers. I have triggers. For some coming out of high-pressure Christianity, being asked to share your faith is a trigger, and I respect that—sincerely.

Having said that, a church plant will not take off if people are unwilling to talk about their faith or invite people to church. So, while you need to have respect and compassion for those who have triggers, you also have to find a new way to talk about sharing your faith.

Having grown up in an evangelical setting, I thought we'd start by looking at some stereotypical verses used to challenge people to engage in evangelism. To start, I went to the internet and did a search:

What are some good verses to encourage people to share their faith?

I was not disappointed with the results; it was a treasure of verses, including the Great Commission from the Gospel of Matthew, John 3:16, or Paul's thoughts on sharing our faith in Romans 10:14-15, but one stood out more than any other.

For those with a similar religious history, you might know this verse as well. Here it is:

> Always be prepared to give an answer to everyone who asks you to give the reason for the hope that you have. (1 Peter 3:15)

Did you ever have to memorize this verse? You know, it's not so bad. It's kind of a nice verse, for those of us not triggered. *If you are filled with hope, you should tell people about it!* That doesn't sound so bad.

So, let's reconsider it, this time without the unhealthy assumptions attached to it.

This verse is attributed to Peter and was written to the church when the church was small and spread out. Christianity was not a major religion as it is today. It was a small cult or sect of Judaism, and because it was new and small, it was not well respected by the general population. In fact, it was generally hated, feared, and misunderstood. Most new things are—and if you plant a church, you will experience this firsthand. People tend to hate and fear—or are generally suspicious of—things they don't understand.

This conflict is the major focus of Peter's letter. He's writing to a church that is small, the minority in a world surrounded by powerful empires and religions; a church that was hated by everyone else. This is important to realize, because Peter's letter was written for Christians when they were the minority, and the things he says are really helpful for Christians who are cast aside and looked down on. But that means, bringing his lessons into modern day America does require some interpretation. Christians are not a minority in America.

Many of our major national holidays are *Christian* holidays (or *holy days*, as the word origin would note). That is not the case for other religions in America, and that was certainly not the case for the early Christians. When Peter wrote this letter, the kids in the church did not get off school for Easter or Christmas. They weren't bringing cards for St. Valentine's Day or wearing green on St. Patrick's Day. And no one was celebrating All Hollow's Eve, the night before All Saints Day.

Estimates from 2021 suggest that of the entire US population, or 332 million, as much as 63% identifies as Christian, or around 210 million.

In other words: this letter was not written with us in mind. This was written for Christians who numbered 12 to 50 people in a city of a million. It was written when Christians were so small, the only people who knew about them found them annoying.

In other words, it wasn't written for us, but that doesn't mean people today can't learn something from it. Be careful not to over identify. In America, Christians must learn to distinguish between the grief that comes from losing our influence and power in society, and actual persecution. So, when it talks about persecution, let's remember what it was referring to.

Don't worry, even with the responsibility to properly interpret, there's still lots of good advice in this letter. Here is one such piece of advice.

> Conduct yourselves honorably among the Gentiles. (1 Peter 2:12)

Christians, in a time when they were the minority, were told to show everyone else living around them respect. To treat them with honor, or to hold people outside the faith in high esteem. If when Christians are living in a place where they are the minority, they are expected to treat other people outside the faith with respect, how much more should we?

That sounds like a pretty good place to start when it comes to sharing our faith.

So, with all of this in mind, let's look at our verse as it sits in this letter, and see if it lines up with what we've learned already. 1 Peter 3, starting with verse 8 says this:

> Finally, all of you, be like-minded, be sympathetic, love one another, be compassionate and humble.

Interesting way to start, Peter. Imagine if Christians took *this* verse seriously? Why weren't evangelicals asked to memorize *this* verse? Or at least taught this verse in relation to sharing your faith? Peter goes on:

> Do not repay evil with evil or insult with insult. On the contrary, repay evil with blessing, because to this you were called so that you may inherit a blessing. (1 Peter 3:8-9)

To a world where Christians were surrounded by people who looked down on them, spit on them, thoughtless of them, Peter says: don't treat others the way you've been treated. Get back at people by blessing them.

The whole world was against them, but in Jesus, they were not to be against the world.

Here's the first lesson in sharing our faith, and it's an important lesson you should never forget.

You *share* your faith by being a blessing to others who don't *share* your faith. In fact, scripture makes this clear over and over again. If you bless others, it's only then that *you* will inherit a blessing. You share our faith, not in an attempt to convert someone, but in an attempt to bless them.

Peter goes on, and here, he does what many early Christians do. He's writing in a time when there wasn't a New Testament. All they had was the Old Testament, so if they wanted to really drive a point home, they had to quote the Hebrew Bible.

Peter quotes Psalms:

> Whoever would love life
> and see good days
> must keep their tongue from evil
> and their lips from deceitful speech.
> They must turn from evil and do good;
> they must seek peace and pursue it.
> For the eyes of the Lord are on the righteous
> and his ears are attentive to their prayer,
> but the face of the Lord is against those who do evil.
> (1 Peter 3:10-12)

If you read the rest of this Psalm, it's the one that says, "Taste and see that the Lord is good" (Psalm 34:8). Of all the passages drilled into me about sharing my faith, I still love that one the most.

If people give God a try, they won't be disappointed.

This Psalm has a lot of other things to say as well. It says if you want to see things work out—if you want "good days" or if you want to really love your life—there are some things you should do and some things you shouldn't do.

You shouldn't lie or trick people. Seems obvious, but still good advice. Instead, you *should seek peace*—shalom, the well-being of all people. Seek peace: go after the overall well-being of society. You do that, and life will be good for everyone.

It's pretty simple logic. Do you want "the good life"? Easy. Do good in the world and the world will be better for everyone. By blessing others, you will bless yourself, because by making the world a better place you will be making the world a better place for yourself as well. And isn't that what everyone wants, regardless of their faith or worldview? Don't atheists, agnostics, Christians, Muslims, Mormons, church people, and non-church people all want our community to be better? Doesn't everyone want safer neighborhoods, better homes, and a nicer place to raise their family?

This is exactly what Peter is getting at in chapter 3, verse 13:

> Who is going to harm you if you are eager to do good?

No one is going to be mad at you if you're trying to make the world a better place.

People will forgive you for being a Christian, if they believe that you honestly want to do good things in the world and you're not going to be judgmental about it.

Who is going to harm you if you are eager to do good?

Who is going to argue with you if you actually want to be a blessing, with no strings attached?

Growing Generous Givers

Often people like to put limits on who is expected to give. I was at a church where they were doing a fundraiser, and there was an adult with a disability there. One of the leaders went up to them and told them to ignore the presentation; it wasn't for them. I'm confident they did this out of a desire to help this person not feel pressured, but I fear this kind of comment does more to belittle than empower. Being generous isn't about having a lot, it's about giving what you can. One of the most empowering things a person can do is give something away. We have lots of adults with disabilities in our church and they always leave some change in the offering. Don't take that away. Celebrate it! Be careful not to limit who you encourage to give, regardless of who they are or what they believe. Whether someone is a Christian or an atheist, people are looking for places to be generous.

It's only after Peter writes all of this that he gets to saying this:

> Always be prepared to give an answer to everyone who asks you to give the reason for the hope that you have. (1 Peter 3:15)

For Peter, it's all about hope. He doesn't say, "Always be ready to give a theological dissertation for every argument against our faith" or "Always be ready to argue with everyone about what you believe." He says: be ready for when people ask about your hope.

One of the teens in our church got a call from a friend from school. The friend said, "I didn't grow up Christian, and my parents aren't religious, but I could really use some hope in my life. Would you be willing to tell me more about Jesus?"

A member of our church has a friend who identifies as pagan. Recently she reached out to someone at church and asked if she could learn more about our faith. She has always been pagan but said she needs something a little more *hopeful* in her life and thinks she could probably put up with some of the teachings of Jesus. A growing number of young people are growing up with non-religious questions and they are looking for places to have safe conversations about faith. If you're building a community of hope, free from judgment, people will come to your church looking for answers.

Hope is the belief that things could be better for everyone.

Hope is the belief that, through God, things will work out.

Hope is the belief that no matter what someone is going through, no matter how bad it's gotten, there's a chance, things could work out—for everyone.

Couldn't everyone use a little bit of hope? Peter seems to think so. Read it again.

> Always be prepared to give an answer to everyone who asks you to give the reason for the hope that you have. (1 Peter 3:15 NIV)

You have to be ready to share this hope with eagerness. "Always" and with "everyone"—not just with the people you like. Not just with the people who agree with you. Not just with the people who believe the same thing as you. No, share your hope with everyone, *always*, and he doesn't leave it there, just in case we're confused.

> But do this with gentleness and respect… (1 Peter 3:16a NIV)

With gentleness and respect? Synonyms for gentleness include kindness, tenderness, mercy, carefulness. Synonyms for respect include appreciation, dignity, esteem, honor, recognition.

It's funny how that part often gets left off. When you talk about what you believe, you should do it carefully and with respect and gentleness.

Chapter 9

A Thought Experiment

Consider a hypothetical situation between you and a Muslim who happens to be your neighbor, but in this situation, you're not sharing *your* faith with *them*. They are sharing *their* faith with *you*.

So, imagine with me. You have a neighbor who is Muslim, and you've become friends. They know you're a Christian, and you know they are a Muslim. You hang out with this neighbor—you go to each other's houses, have cookouts, see each other when taking the trash out, and watch out for each other's kids when they are playing in your cul-de-sac. One day, when sitting in your backyard, around your fire pit, with the kids running around in a post-smore's sugar high, your neighbor starts talking about what they believe.

Your friend shares their faith with you, and at first you get nervous.

Are they going to try and convert you?

No. Whew. They aren't trying to make you a Muslim. You can relax.

They are just sharing something that is important to them. They talk casually about: what they believe, why they believe it, what it means to them.

In this hypothetical situation, how would you respond?

Would you be interested?

Would you enjoy hearing about what your Muslim friend believes?

Would you be curious and ask questions?

Of course you would! There's no better way to show someone you care than with honest curiosity.

So, you keep hanging out, and this time, you're standing at your fence, chatting about each other's yards, when they bring up their mosque and the landscaping they help do there. This starts you down a whole rabbit trail of how much they love their mosque. It turns out they go almost every week. They volunteer in their teen program, raising up the next generation of Muslims. They enjoy volunteering with the teens but really love some of the community service their mosque does, and that they can use their love of landscaping to keep the grounds nice.

They tell you stories of life at the mosque.

Would you listen?

Would you enjoy hearing about this?

Would you be glad they trusted you enough to share this part of their life with you?

Why not?!

Now, to be fair, you might be curious—and you have a right to be. After a few more conversations, you might want to know how they feel about LGBTQ+ people. Or women: Do they allow women to lead? What are their stances on other topics or doctrine that are important to you? You can already assume, from what you heard, that they aren't like the extreme Muslims you read about or the two-dimensional caricatures you've seen in movies.

You can tell they love everyone, and they believe Allah loves everyone.

Would you find that fascinating?

Maybe even a little encouraging?

Would you be glad they talked to you about these things?

Would this be meaningful to you?

More importantly, would you be able to separate what they believe from the stereotypes you've heard or experienced? Or would you only be able to see them as the Muslims you've been raised to question?

Maybe they will go on to tell you about how their mosque is holding a really special event that they're really excited about, and they mention it would be fun to have you come along—but no pressure of course.

Would you consider going?

Would you be insulted or annoyed they invited you?

Or would you be honored they felt safe enough with you to ask you to join them at their place of worship?

Think about this hypothetical situation and ask yourself: If you could imagine yourself enjoying a conversation where you hear about another person's faith, can you imagine yourself, or the members of your church, enjoying a conversation where you share your faith?

And more specifically, what are you robbing your friends of experiencing if you or your members avoid sharing your faith?

A good friend, who cares about you and who approaches life with curiosity, isn't going to judge you for believing something. They might even find it interesting.

To be fair, Christians have done a lot to be ashamed of but so has every other religion in the world. You can't carry the responsibility of every other Christian, religion, or person of faith, any more than you should expect your neighbor to. You would never put that on another person—you would never blame your Muslim neighbor for what other Muslims have done. So don't do it to yourself either.

There are many Christians, Muslims, Buddhists, and every other worldview in the world that has done violent things. They have all been horrible at times, but whatever you believe—whatever your neighbor believes—as long as you're committed to love, you have nothing to be ashamed of. In fact, your friends might be excited to hear you're not like other radical versions of Christianity—that you love everyone. That you believe God loves everyone. That you believe women can lead and LGBTQ+ people can fully participate in the life of the church. They might love to hear something like that.

It might just give them hope, and couldn't everyone use a little bit of hope?

This hypothetical story is meant to help you loosen up and become more comfortable sharing your faith, especially if you have struggled with the mistakes Christians have made, and you have over-identified with the mistakes of other people who claim to be followers of Jesus. Thinking through this situation can help let go of those expectations and be more honest, in a non-threatening way, about what you believe and why it is important to you.

Whether this thought experiment helps you or not isn't the point. The point is that you won't be able to plant a church while doing everything you can to hide what you believe. You must find an authentic and sincere way to reclaim evangelism.

As a church planter, you not only have to be willing to talk about what you believe, but you have to find ways to teach your launch team to do the same. You must find a way to help people who are struggling with triggers and shame realize that they don't have to carry the blame for what others have done in Jesus's name. You can trust that good, caring, curious people will see you for who you are, not who they associate you with or the negative stereotypes they watch on the news.

Testimonies

A good first step in getting people to share their faith out in the world, is to create space for them to share their faith with each other. There is nothing more powerful than to hear people's stories of faith.

It helps people think about what they believe, it creates connection and community as people hear each other's stories, and it helps people learn how to talk about who they are.

When I was planting, one of my coaches was Christian Coon, co-founder of Urban Village Church in Chicago. Urban Village set out to be an inclusive space that was intentional about reclaiming evangelism. As part of this mission, they created space in every worship service for someone to share their story. They use a simple instruction guide for people sharing their story. You can find an updated version of this resource on our toolkit at churchplantershandbook.org/.

It can do a lot for a new church for people to share their stories. Take time in worship or in launch team meetings so that people are more comfortable discussing who they are and what they believe. This will make inviting people to church a hundred times easier.

Chapter 10

Marketing & Branding

My wife and I go out to eat often. We have our favorites, but occasionally we try new things. While people have offered us all kinds of suggestions in the past, I have short-term memory issues, and even now, as I write, I can't remember any of the restaurants that people have recommended to me. *Why would I remember them?* I don't need to.

When I'm interested in finding a new place to try out, I go to a search engine and I look for a place to eat, narrowing my search to what's open, and what neighborhood I'm interested in driving to. Then I will read the reviews, check the prices, and, as I narrow my options, look at the menu. I can tell, from most restaurants' online presence, whether I want to go there to eat or not before ever leaving my house. Since this has worked well for me, I've trained my brain to no longer remember people's personal recommendations.

This is a product of our technology. With each new technological age, humans begin to use their brains differently. Neil Postman in his book *Technopoly* shares Plato's story of the invention of writing.[1] In this fable, the inventor of writing was convinced it would improve one's memory. He shared his invention with the local king, but the king was wise enough to know it would do the opposite. He interrupts and says to the inventor:

> The discoverer of an art is not the best judge of the good or harm which will accrue to those who practice it. So, it is in this: you, who are the father of writing, have out of fondness for your off-spring attributed to it quite the opposite of its real function. Those who acquire it will cease to exercise their memory and become forgetful; they will rely on writing to bring things to their remembrance by external signs instead of by their own internal resources.

If you're able to write something down, you no longer need to remember it. Technology shapes how our minds work, and this truth applies to every invention since the invention of writing. It has significant ramifications for the modern church. If you're able to get on the internet, and find a church, the service times, read their statement of faith, and sample a few sermons, it won't matter who recommended the church—you'll know for yourself whether it's a good fit.

In other words, personal invites are often as good as the digital presence to back them up.

Consider someone invites you to church, but before you go, you do some research, and you can't tell if the church loves gay people, and you happen to be gay—will you go? Maybe you've tried a dozen churches already and you've learned that if a church doesn't say it's inclusive clearly on the website, it probably isn't. So, you do the only reasonable thing: you stay home. In situations like this, it won't matter how great the recommendation your friend made. In fact, if they recommended a church, knowing all along that the church doesn't accept their friend for who God made them to be, it might do more to harm the friendship than anything else.

Personal invitations are important—they are essential. Multiple chapters discussed the importance of meeting new people and reclaiming evangelism. But often, when a friend invites someone and they become interested, they are likely to look up the church online, read about it, and decide for themselves if the recommendation matches what they want in a church.

What you say about your church online your values, theology, sermons—matters.

The number one reason someone finds a church is because someone they know invited them. According to a 2016 Pew Research poll, when looking for a new church "roughly seven-in-ten talked to members of the congregation (69%) or to friends or colleagues (68%) about the house of worship they were considering. Upward of half of those searching for a new house of worship talked to a minister or clergyperson (55%). Fewer say they looked for information online (37%)."[2] At first glance, and with only the total numbers laid out, 37% looking for information online doesn't seem that high. That is until you consider how these percentages change when you take age into account. When only considering those under the age of 30, it jumps from 37% to 59%—that's only 10% less than someone talking to them about it. And this was back in 2016: before COVID, before everything moved online, and before TikTok. This percentage will only increase. Digital natives will increasingly look things up before they show up.

Clear Is Kind

Many seeker-friendly evangelical churches maintain an ambiguous stance on LGBTQ+ inclusion, which means their public messaging often avoids direct statements about their stance. Their hope is to attract people, regardless of orientation, and many generally believe that God will take care of the rest. It's only after they get involved that people will find out their policies around LGBTQ+.

Marketing from this vantage is not only damaging, but it also doesn't work.

When a church presents itself as welcoming without disclosing deeper convictions, it risks not only ethical compromise, but it will also only contribute to the harm being done. People are perceptive; eventually, they will uncover the truth. When they do, many will leave, or worse, try to conform. Ambiguity amplifies, in all facets of relationships. Clear is kind.

The goal in marketing a church isn't to trick someone into visiting so you can convert them into the image of what you think they should be. The goal in marketing is to clearly communicate who you are, who you are striving to be, and what it means for someone to be a part of your community so they can decide for themselves if it's a good fit. It's only then that those who are looking for what you have to offer are going to be able to find you.

Jesus tells us this is what the kingdom of heaven will be like, in Matthew 13:44-46:

> The kingdom of heaven is like treasure hidden in a field. When a man found it, he hid it again, and then in his joy went and sold all he had and bought that field.
>
> Again, the kingdom of heaven is like a merchant looking for fine pearls. When he found one of great value, he went away and sold everything he had and bought it.

Christians often talk about the idea that God goes after the lost—the lost sheep, the lost coin, the lost son. The theology is rich with grace and paints a beautiful picture of God's grace. But that is not what's being discussed in these passages. Here, it's the kingdom of God that's hidden and there are those who are eagerly searching for it. People are searching for what God has to offer, and good and ethical marketing helps people find what they are looking for.

The last thing you want to do is attract people with a treasure chest, only for them to open it and find it filled with cobwebs or a fake pearl.

Don't pretend to be something you're not.

Marketing with integrity respects the dignity of choice. This kind of marketing believes that people can choose for themselves what is best for them, and you're not trying to persuade them, you're trying to provide the best, most accurate positive information you can about your church so that those who are looking for that kind of church will find it.

Edit As You Go Along

Remember, iteration is one of the key tools in the church planter's toolbox.

When we launched our first church, we were trying to do something new, while still competing with the more popular churches in our community, and this reality was reflected in how we talked about ourselves online. Our website painted a picture of our church based on what we were competing against instead of who we were trying to be. I remember meeting a visitor within the first couple of months of launching who regularly attended one of the largest churches in our city. They decided to give our church plant a try, since it was closer to where they lived. If they could get the same experience with less travel, it'd be win-win. I knew as soon as they started talking, they were going to be disappointed. We didn't have a light show, and we didn't play behind a bed of music. We didn't even dim the lights.

Later that day, I was reading through the connect cards, and a visitor offered feedback, and I knew it had to be the same person—we didn't have very many visitors that day. They recommended we dim the lights in the worship area, use more lights on the stage, and include a bed of music throughout worship to help create a more "worshipful" environment.

They were describing the large church they usually attended; they thought we'd be more effective if we were more like them. That's when I realized that they had come to our church hoping we'd be more of a performance, even though *we were intentionally* trying to do the opposite. They said they found us online, so I knew they came to our church *because of our website*. What about our website gave them the impression we wanted to be another performance-driven church?

When interactions like this occur, and people show up to your church expecting one thing but experiencing something different, it's important to properly debrief. Do you need to improve the experience? Or do you need to clarify the expectation? Engage in reverse engineering to help clarify who you are and what people can expect.

Assuming you don't need to tweak the experience, and you're reaching people who looked you up online, scour your website.

When someone visits and it's clearly not what they are looking for, ask yourself: *What about our digital presence made them think we'd be this way?* Then scour your website and adjust. With a fresh pair of eyes, find what part of your language or photos is giving them that impression.

This is a common temptation. When you're desperate to get people through the doors, you'll try to describe your church based on what you think people want, instead of who you are.

As you continue to receive feedback from guests, adjust the website, clarifying to the world who you are and what people can expect. You're not trying to discourage people from coming; you're trying to provide the right information so people can make an informed decision about your community.

You should also ask people who stick around, whether that's informally or at visitor events. *How did you find our church and what kept you coming?* They will tell you what's great about your church in often more concise and accurate ways than any marketing guru can. Take their answers, convert them to taglines and phrases, and plaster them on the site. There's no one who knows how to describe a church better than people who are new. Outsiders can point out what's obvious.

Learning how to be honest about yourself will do a lot to help people find you online. In time, after proper iteration, you will meet visitors who are looking for a church exactly like yours! Your visitor retention will go up and people who visit will come back multiple times. Why? Because the people who are looking for a church like yours are able to find you.

Clarify Your Message

Here are some examples of how to clarify common phrases used on a church website.

"We're offering contemporary worship and relevant messages."

First, every church plant in America claims to do the same, so it's not very original. Second, are you *really*? If someone tunes into your "contemporary" worship service and you're singing "Shout to the Lord," please don't advertise yourself as contemporary. That song was written in 1993. Hymns have aged better than "Shout to the Lord."

Simply put, some things don't age as well as others. It's why wood paneling from the 1970s isn't as popular as hardwood floors from 100-year-old homes. A "contemporary" house would be amazing with 100-year-old, reclaimed hardwood floors, but one with a room of cheap wood paneling lining the walls isn't going to move as quickly. That's the hard thing about contemporary music; it has a short lifespan. This doesn't mean you shouldn't use contemporary music. According to Tony Morgan, from the Unstuck Group, most growing churches "are more likely to offer modern/contemporary worship than declining churches."[3] Whatever you do, be sure it's clearly communicated. If you're claiming to do contemporary worship, then do modern songs.

"We're a reconciling congregation."

Great! But did you know this is a very insider way of telling people you're inclusive? "Reconciling" is the United Methodist term referring to LGBTQ+ inclusion. But the United Church of Christ uses the phrase Open and Affirming, which is often referred to as ONA. The Presbyterians call it "more light." The ministries behind each of these labels are wonderful testimonies to the power of social justice advocacy. At the same time, they are primarily insider-terms, used to promote institutional change. People outside these denominations—the people you're trying to reach—may or may not know what *ONA*, *reconciling*, or *more light* means. Words like *inclusion*, *affirming*, or a pride flag will do more to make your point clear.

When necessary, define what you mean, so there's no ambiguity.

"We're going to change the world!"

What a job to take on! How exactly do you plan on changing the world? And by "world," do you mean the entire world? Don't make your mission sound more than it is. Be specific, and when possible, keep it local.

A few other ways to say this to make it more accurate would be "We're invested in making a change in the 43223 zip code" or "We're hoping to change our city."

Don't make your mission sound better than it is.

"God called us to save the lost in this city."

Well, besides the fact that it's unclear what you mean by "lost" the general tone of this is insulting.

Who said the "lost" wanted saving?

Be careful not to insult the people you hope to connect with.

"We're a growing church."

Often churches use "growing" to describe the wishful thinking of a church smaller than it wants to be. It's as if "small" is seen as a derogatory word and must be avoided. The truth is that many people are looking for small churches. They've been to the mega churches, got lost in the crowds, and are looking for something different. If you avoid this word in your descriptions, you make it all the harder for them to find you in their online search. If you're a small church, it's ok to say that. Keep it positive. Refuse to let accurate descriptions of yourself be seen as negative—a good lesson in life as well as church.

There's nothing wrong with being small.

Don't sell yourself short.

"We hope to have a youth ministry someday."

That's great! The same sentiment could be made for any ministry: *a worship band, choir, children's ministry, permanent location… fill in the blank.* The question isn't whether you'd like to have that someday, but do you have a plan for making these things a reality? If all you mean by that statement is that you're hoping someday it works out, but you don't have a plan in place, be honest about that.

Don't give people the impression you will do something if you don't have a plan to make it a reality. If you're not careful, false promises like this can be used to try to convince visitors to stay. Be honest.

There could be endless other examples. The goal is to refine your language on your website and social media profiles, editing your taglines and descriptions, so that those looking for a church like yours can find you.

Be Generous

Your launch team will be your biggest billboards. Don't make them pay for stuff. If you design a shirt with your church's logo and name, give it away. Launch team members will be more likely to wear it and tell people about their church if it's high quality, well-designed, and *free*! The same for anything else you can give away: water bottles, car decals, coffee mugs, tumblers, or stickers. Give stuff away with your church's name and logo on it, and it will not only help people learn about your church but model the value of being generous.

Growing Generous Givers

Lots of churches charge for every interaction. People must buy a book to participate in the Bible study or give a suggested donation to eat at the community dinner, or purchase a shirt with the church logo on it. While all of these are fine in certain situations, when a church is launching, and you're trying to build a culture of generosity, give away as much as you can. When churches charge for these things, they lose more than they make. When we turn church into a transaction, taking someone's money in exchange for a product, they are made to believe that they have contributed to the church. Purchasing merchandise is how people support businesses and so it's only natural to think of supporting a church this way. But a church isn't a business. It's a community funded by the generosity of its members. By withholding these kinds of transactions and encouraging people to be generous, you are teaching them what it means to truly contribute to the church. Not only does it avoid the church becoming a transaction, but people are invited to participate in the economy of abundance.

Representation Matters

Consider doing a little experiment. Go to a church website—find a popular one in town. Look at their front page. What kind of photos are present? Is it diverse? Are there women and men? Children and young people? Make a note and then click into their website. Try to find their list of pastors, board members, or campus pastors. Is the diversity of the leaders matched by the diversity of their community?

If you build your church website with a photo of people of color, women, minorities, and young people on the front page, there better be just as many in your list of staff, pastors, and board members.

Representation matters, especially for your digital presence, but only if it matches your leadership structure.

If your church has women in leadership, highlight that on your website! In a world where women are discouraged to lead, having a church where they can, stands out. Whoever is leading in your church, celebrate it. On most websites, the staff/board webpage remains in the top three most visited pages on a site. When someone is looking for a church, they want to know who's leading it. Which means, whatever you claim to be, whether it's diverse or LGBTQ+ friendly, or anything else, there should be *representation in your leadership.*

Representation is more than just choosing diverse stock photos. It's about putting people into leadership and allowing your community to be influenced by their gifts, talents, and perspectives.

The Medium Is the Message

Every year, our neighborhood shuts down the street and hosts a massive neighborhood block party. There are food trucks, vendors, and live music and every year since before we launched, we've purchased a spot to set up a table.

It's been a great way to connect with new people.

This year, we were brainstorming how we might increase our interactions at this event. It was a particularly hot summer, and we thought it'd be great to pass out cold water. Since we try to be environmentally friendly, I suggested we buy branded reusable plastic bottles and have ice water for people to fill the water bottle with. There really are no free water sources available at the event.

I shared this with one of our staff members, and they felt that even buying plastic bottles, even if reusable, still wasn't in line with our values. She suggested stainless steel bottles, which are better for the environment. As I did research, I found stainless steel bottles would be out of our price range. That's when I discovered bottles made from sugar cane, a more environmentally friendly product than traditional plastic at a similar price tag.

Now we can pass out environmentally friendly water bottles, with our logo, and provide ice cold water to people walking by.

The idea of giving away water was a great idea, but it had to be done in a way that lined up with our values.

When marketing a church, remember the age-old communication principle: **the medium is the message.**[4] The *kind* of water bottle you give away says as much about you as the message on the water bottle. The same principle applies in all your marketing.

Imagine giving away 1,000 stickers at a community event. The *message* on them says "God loves you." Now, imagine those stickers are low quality, smear when getting wet, hard to peel off, or tear easily. The sticker is the *medium,* and if it's low quality, that will say more about how your church and what you think about God's love than the message written on it ever will.

Let's say your church loves to host meals for your congregation and your neighbors. When you host a meal for your congregation, it's catered and includes lots of sides. But when you host a meal for your neighbors living in poverty, it's simple sandwiches and no sides. The message is a free meal, but the medium you choose based on the audience will tell the wider community how you really feel about them.

When giving something away, be sure it reflects the quality and values you hope to communicate.

Remember, *the medium is the message.*

A Brief Word About Branding

There's nothing more exciting than a new brand! Which is why it's important you find a professional to help you develop your brand. Having a clean, professional, modern brand is essential to connecting with new people. But getting a logo and brand is only the first step. The second is learning how to use it. A great brand, misused, will be a waste of money.

Here's the secret to using a brand effectively. A brand includes four essential elements, and a professional graphic designer will provide you with each of these and give you examples of how to use them:

1. **Logo**: It needs to be clean, professional, and versatile, including options in color, grayscale, and monochromatic settings.
2. **Colors**: A brand will include 3-5 colors that will be incorporated into the logo, website, print materials, outdoor signage, and anything else with your brand. Often, there is a shade of black, a shade of white, a main color, and an accent color. The shades of black and white are used for background and text. The main color is used for headings, buttons, the logo, etc. The accent color is used anytime you need to have something stand out. Everything you put out there, whether it's a website, brochure, or podcast, should be using these exact colors to ensure your brand is consistent. There's no reason to use any other colors on official marketing materials.
3. **Fonts**: In general, you need a font for a heading and one for the body of the text. Once again, every piece of official church communication materials should consistently use these two fonts, from websites, to letterhead, to signage, to printed brochures. Using a consistent font and color on all your printed and digital materials will do more to create a consistent brand than any logo can by itself.
4. **Textures and Background**: A good brand kit will show you how to use the logo, colors, and fonts with various backgrounds and textures. Stick to these backgrounds and textures throughout your materials.

The best advice you can receive for using a brand well is to avoid being too creative. Brands are effective because they are consistent. There's no need to use additional fonts, creative backgrounds, or new colors. Keep things consistent on all official communications for your church.

Marketing Essentials

From developing an online presence, to increasing location-based searches, here is a list of tools you can use to help tell your story.

1. **Website**: Your website is the front door to your church and worth having designed by a professional. A good church website should be clean and easy to navigate, with plenty of margin and white space to enhance readability. It should include a clear call to action—whether that's visiting a service, getting involved, or learning more. Essential information for visitors should be easy to find, such as service times, location, parking details, and what to expect. Sample teachings or sermons should be accessible for those exploring the church's message. A staff or leadership page helps build connection, and there should be an easy way to contact someone, whether through a contact form, email, or phone number.
2. **Email marketing:** Find a service that will allow you to collect, store, and email long lists of subscribers. It's important that this is more than a list in your personal email. By using a professional email service, you can create sign-up forms to gather passive subscribers and design emails that look professional. Also, professional services follow best practices, allowing people to unsubscribe from your list if they want. Sending a monthly newsletter to your entire list is a great way to keep everyone in your church informed.
3. **Text messaging:** There are great text messaging services. While you don't want to overuse this method, this can be effective in moderation, whether it's reminding people of your Launch Day or other important events.
4. **Social media**: Find the social media platforms that make sense for your target audience. In general, it's best to start with one platform and build that slowly. You can always add additional platforms later. Having one consistent platform is far better than having multiple inactive platforms. You might also consider using a social media publishing program to post to multiple platforms at once.
5. **Maps (Apple/Google)**: When people are looking for a church, just like when they are looking for a restaurant, they often search within a specific geographic area. It's extremely important to create business profiles for all major map services so you can manage and update

them with all relevant information, respond to requests, and allow people to leave reviews.

6. **Reviews**: Before you launch, ask your launch team to complete a review on Google, Facebook, Apple, Yelp, or anywhere else you see the most traffic. When searching for something, people read the reviews.
7. **Local news:** In the chapter on catalytic events, we discuss more ways to get the local news to share your story.
8. **Door-to-Door:** Often, church plants walk around hanging door hangers or leaving gifts on the doors of those closest to the church. Be sure to follow local codes and expectations—the last thing you want to be is a bad neighbor.
9. **Community festival and events:** If there's a prominent community event already happening, be sure to be a part of it. This might mean offering volunteers, setting up a table, or sponsoring the event.
10. **Invite cards:** Design great looking business cards that launch teams can use to pass out to their friends.
11. **Mailer**: Sending people something in the mail can stand out and is a great way to connect with people close to your location. In 2016, ARC, a prominent evangelical church planting network, suggested spending $10,000 on a mailer. In 2021, these numbers remained the same, telling their pastors to do one mailer to at least 100,000 addresses. They claim that the key to a successful mailer is doing it once and going as big as you can, directing people to a key event. This only works if you have a strong digital presence, great website with a clear call to action, and effective outreach that matches your mailer invite. With the right digital and outreach processes in place, the national return is around .0025, which means if you send 100,000 mailers, you can hope for around 250 on your Launch Sunday. If you send out 60,000 mailers, you can hope for around 150, and if you send only 5,000 mailers, you will be lucky if you have 12 visitors.[5] This goes back to the input/output conversation. The input it takes is always greater than we think. We must be willing to put everything into this if we want to see the results.

12. **Social media advertising**: It's worth paying for social media ads, but it's worth being careful how these ads are set up. Carefully choose your audience, geographic area, and purpose of the ads. For example, there's no need to advertise your church to people looking for one in the next state over (unless it's an online church), and there's no need to share about your inclusive church to people who don't think the church should be—unless that's your goal. "Engagement" in social media terms means anyone who comments or interacts with a post. As far as social media is concerned, there is not a value attached to those engagements. Someone who disagrees with your inclusion is more likely to comment on your post than someone who agrees with it. So, if you're not careful in setting your ad parameters, it's easier for social media to get the promised "engagements" by putting it in front of people who are the opposite of your target audience. You're paying for each click, so be sure those clicks are potential visitors and not the opposite.

Tips on Saving Money on Marketing

Marketing costs money, and in a world of declining churches, it will be tempting to make cuts wherever you can. This is especially common for mainline churches that are not used to investing in large outreach or marketing endeavors. Every church plant model is different and if your model leans heavily into grassroots volunteer lay pastors who work full-time jobs outside the church, you will become sustainable sooner. But if your model is hoping to afford a full-time pastor, with benefits, and staff in the next 3-5 years, you will need to invest money to make it happen. **Don't be afraid to spend money.**

You will need to be comfortable spending $10,000 on a single mailer. It's a big risk and it needs to be designed well, but there are kinds of risks that produce positive results.

This is true not only for marketing but every step of the way, including your location and set-up supplies. A church launching in rented space might spend up to $40,000 on a trailer and portable church equipment and then another $30,000 to $50,000 a year on rent. In the scarcity mindset, where the world has only limited resources and the church must hoard everything, this could feel like a waste. Yet, in the economy of abundance, this is an investment.

When it comes to fundraising, people give to things they care about. The atmosphere, accessibility, and practical use of your gathering space to accomplish your church's mission is something donors are willing to invest in. The same is true for marketing and reaching new people. If you try to spend less out of a scarcity mindset, people will donate less, following the church's example. While you need to be good stewards of the resources you have, you also need to be willing to take risks financially, trusting God to provide. This kind of God-honoring risk can inspire your donors to do the same. In a backwards sort of way, spending money strategically (and learning to tell the story) will help you raise more money. On the other hand, hoarding discourages giving.

While you will need to spend money, it's always great to save money where you can. Here are a few ways for registered nonprofits, including churches, to save money:

1. **Google for Nonprofits:** Through this program, you can create free church-branded emails for your organization and receive free ad grants. This will put your church in front of people looking for churches on Google for free as if it were a paid promotion.
2. **Techsoup:** This service allows you to access a host of discounted programs and subscriptions, including Microsoft Office 360, Adobe Design Suite, Quickbooks Online, and more. It's easy to register with your tax-exempt status and when you do, your church will save thousands of dollars every year.
3. **Canva for Nonprofits**: Canva offers a subscription for eligible nonprofits, allowing access to premium design tools for creating social media graphics, flyers, and presentations.
4. **Mailchimp Nonprofit Discount**: If your church uses email marketing, Mailchimp offers discounts for nonprofits. This service helps you manage newsletters and outreach effectively.

5. **YouTube Nonprofit Program**: Get access to special features, including donation buttons and enhanced video tools, to help expand your church's online presence.

Church Planter's Toolkit

Go to churchplantershandbook.org to access the following resources related to this chapter:

- **Choosing the Right Name for Your Church:** If you're still struggling on a name, or wondering if it will be effective in marketing, use this guide.
- **"Tell Better Stories" eBook:** This short eBook lays out the basics of effective storytelling.
- **Ten Tips for an Effective Website:** Whether you're doing it yourself or hiring a professional, this simple guide will help you get started.
- **How to Use a Brand Correctly:** Having a brand designed professionally is just the first step. Download this guide to ensure you're using it to its full potential.
- **Marketing Essentials Checklist:** Download this simple checklist to track how your marketing strategy is going.

Chapter 11

Location, Location, Location

You know you're a church planter when you enter a space you can't help but imagine what it would take to hold a church gathering there. If this isn't something you do already, give it a try! Every time you enter a space—whether it's a restaurant, coffee house, event space, conference center, theater, school—take time to ponder: What would it take to turn this into a location for a new church? Where would the preacher stand? How would we do music? Is there room for a band? Would people sit in rows or around tables? Would the entrance be obvious? Is there enough parking? Is there space for children's ministry? Would people outside the church feel comfortable in this space? This is a great exercise to do regularly. Stretching your creative muscles in this way will help you train your eyes to see new God-possibilities.

No matter where you meet, there is one thing that remains constant. God is with you. As scripture says in 2 Samuel 7:6:

> I have not dwelt in a house from the day I brought the Israelites up out of Egypt to this day. I have been moving from place to place with a tent as my dwelling.

Like the tabernacle in the times of the Hebrew people wandering in the wilderness, it's not about *where* you met for worship, but the God who meets you there.

As Jesus promises, "For where two or three are gathered in my name, I'm there with them" (Matthew 18:20).

Be careful how you define a religious space. Theologically, anywhere we gather in Jesus's name *becomes* a religious space.

Chapter 11

A Building Doesn't Equal a Church

In most cities and neighborhoods there is a church *building* on every corner. The idea of having another church in the neighborhood feels excessive to many and is often a constant concern of established churches, impacting a church planter's possibilities. "Why are we planting churches? We should revitalize the existing churches!"

It's more complicated than that. Often historic denominations will only plant a church if an existing church in that neighborhood has closed or is struggling. Church planting is a response to death, instead of an act of life.

For anyone planting within an historic denomination, this will be a place of tension. Knowing the context will help you reframe this in conversations with colleagues and congregations.

To start, let's go back to the beginning of our nation.

In 1820 there was one church for every 875 people. As America grew and expanded and new cities were birthed, leaders planted new churches—a few for every city. From 1860–1906, the ratio grew to one church for every 430 people.[1] As the population grew, the number of churches grew with it!

The church and denominational leaders viewed our nation as a place that was prime for reaching new people with new churches. Those early years of church planting in the US looked a lot like the early church. It was organic, messy, and often done in houses and fields and other public spaces. And it was reaching new people—even young people. In 1906, one-third of the congregations in the US were under the age of twenty-five. From 1776 to 1916, the percentage of people who were religiously affiliated rose from 17%to 53%.[2] America did not *start* as a Christian nation, it *became* a Christian nation—for better or for worse—because of the tireless efforts of church planters.

Then something happened after World War I.

By this time, America had established cities and villages throughout the country, and after there was a church or two in each of these—one on every corner—denominations stopped planting new churches at the same rate they had been. Why plant a church when there is one there already? Why plant something new when the current church seems to be holding steady?

The focus instead turned to helping churches grow larger.[3] From 1906 to 1970 membership in the United Methodist Church grew from 5,252,607 to 10,671,774. This number is deceptive, though, because it gives the illusion that the denomination was growing. And in attendance it was, but from a church planting perspective, the denomination was *shrinking*. While attendance was going up during this time, the number of congregations went from 57,087 to 40,654. Not only did we stop planting churches, but we also started closing them.

Although many efforts have been implemented to reverse this decline, the very thing that resulted in our original growth continues to be a place of tension.

One of the biggest reasons that denominations do not plant new churches is not because of a lack of funding, church planters, or available resources. The biggest reason is fear of upsetting colleagues and congregations who already have a church in that neighborhood. The standard practice for denominations is to only plant churches where one has closed instead of planting one where there is population growth, population change, or church planter's call.

Even though the church is struggling, in years of decline, and the building, while beautiful and well-loved, often has years of deferred maintenance. Even though the building is no longer accessible and the congregation no longer reaches new people, there is an unspoken agreement between denominational leaders and local churches not to plant new churches in the neighborhoods of existing churches. In a great religious irony, existing churches are one of the biggest reasons denominations are cautious about planting new churches in otherwise thriving communities. Theologically and historically, it should be the opposite. Existing churches should be the ones leading the charge to start new churches in their neighborhoods to reach new people. The Fresh Expressions movement in the United Methodist Church is one of the only movements to push established churches in this direction, but more nudges need to be made.

Existing churches need to find a way to embrace the beauty of church planting and offer existing under-utilized buildings to church planters as a resource. This doesn't mean existing church buildings are the ideal place to launch a new church. For numerous reasons, it's often best for a church plant to start somewhere other than a church building. But having a place to hold launch team meetings, store supplies, or office space can make a world of difference for new church start pastors.

At the same time, with proper updates and internal signage, existing church buildings can be a great place for a new church start.

What to Look for in a Potential Facility

The best place to start a new church is in a location that is easy to find, has great parking, appropriate amount of room, and easy to access.

This is why many churches launch inside of schools. According to a 2015 study, "Among new churches who use a school as a meeting space, 74% are self-sufficient within three years."[4] Of all the churches they surveyed, those that launched in a school were the most likely to become self-sustaining. There are many reasons for this. First, large evangelical churches have taken advantage of the availability of schools on Sunday morning. Their large launch model, significant funding, focus on evangelism, and visitor follow-up might influence this more than the actual location. Having said that, a school has a lot to offer that is worth considering. First, it's a public space that everyone is familiar with. People can find schools easily and don't carry specific baggage with a school like they might with a church. Churches have done so well in building spaces that are deeply religious that many people who are not religious are afraid or nervous to enter them. In this way, the church's greatest asset—its religious architecture—becomes a barrier to reaching new people. Schools and other public or nonreligious spaces are better for new churches for this reason. Second, schools usually have lots of flexible space, a great parking lot, and room to set up the space in a variety of ways. In fact, the main barrier to using a school is that it requires an immense amount of set-up and tear-down every week to make it work.

These principles can be applied to a variety of settings, including closed church buildings, theaters, community centers, and more. With the right planning, set-up and updates, and investment, anything is possible.

Whether you use a school, theater, or existing church, here are a few things to keep in mind.

> **Capacity**: Do a full assessment of any potential locations. Consider the number of seats available for adults, the amount of space in the nursery and children's area, and the parking spots. Based on national giving trends and demographic research of the area, you can calculate what you can expect your giving would be in your first year and compare that to the cost of using the space. This will help you launch out of a space that is sustainable. If a location has 150 seats but only enough parking for 70 people, you can expect your average to max at the lowest number. This means you are likely to have a space half empty due to accessibility. When considering capacity, you need to consider not only the seats in the auditorium, but also parking, children's ministry, lobby, etc. You will max out at the lowest number in any of these categories.
>
> **Worship**: Are you doing music, preaching, or something else? Will it be in the round, in rows, or around tables? Will you need a sound system or a kitchen? The answers to these questions dramatically impact what kind of space you might need.
>
> **Children's Ministry:** Will you be offering children's ministry, before, during, or after worship? Where will it be? Does it provide adequate security? Is it safe, clean, and accessible? Where will kids sign in or get dropped off? Where will their parents pick them up? You need space for all of this.
>
> **Lobby/Entrance**: How hard is it to get to your worship space from the parking lot? Do you have a good entrance that can easily connect with visitors to the worship/gathering area? If not, how can greeters and signage help overcome this barrier?

Signage: What signs do you need to ensure everyone knows where to go? In spaces where you have to set up and tear down, you'll want to invest in portable banners and signs that direct people to the right places.

Reputation: How is the building perceived by the community? Is it well-known and easy to find? Will it help create a welcoming environment?

Atmosphere: *The medium is the message*, and that includes the space you gather in. You can tell people God loves them, but if you're saying that in a space that screams something else, it will be hard for them to hear your message. Consider the atmosphere of the space. If you're reaching people hurt by the church, don't launch in a religious environment. Whether it's a theater, art gallery, event center or church, each has its own atmosphere. What does it feel like? How does it smell? We looked at a rental space right next to a veterinary hospital. It smelled like cats. Allyssa, who is allergic, started sneezing after only a few minutes in the space. Is there any natural light or is it all fluorescent lights that buzz overhead? Is it clean or messy? If you're not launching out of a professional space (like a theater, event center, etc.), be sure you do what you can to remove clutter. Churches and other older establishments are often guilty of collecting lots of things that go unnoticed by long-time members. This clutter can do a lot to influence the friendliness and cleanliness of your church.

Be Good Neighbors

When searching for a place to rent, remember that you're not just looking for a venue—you're looking for partners in your mission. One of the best ways to approach potential locations is by seeking out People of peace, individuals who are open to your vision and willing to collaborate. These might be property owners, school administrators, or business leaders with whom you share a connection. Building rapport is essential—take time to learn what they care about, what challenges they face, and how your presence could be a mutual benefit—and always find ways to support shared community endeavors. Trust takes time, and while affordability is important, offering to pay full rates, when necessary, shows integrity and commitment. But you are not just a renter; you are a partner, invested in the well-being of the space and the people who use it. Teach your volunteers to care for the space better than they would their own.

Whatever you do, be a good neighbor.

A local school welcomed a large evangelical church into its theater space. The church paid significant rent, which was a financial lifeline for the under-resourced school district. However, the agreement gave the church complete control of the theater every Sunday morning, making it nearly impossible for the school to host plays or other weekend events. In the end, the students paid the cost. Their opportunities for creative expression and extracurricular activities were limited, all so the church could have an uninterrupted worship space.

Don't be that kind of church plant. Consider the impact of your presence.

Ask questions: How does your use of the space affect the people who rely on it during the rest of the week? Are you making life harder for the very community you hope to serve? A strong church plant isn't just about securing a great location—it's about fostering relationships built on trust, generosity, and genuine care for the people around you.

Chapter 12

Catalytic Events

The great irony of Jesus's mission is that he tried not to garner attention, often rejecting the crowds and telling people to be quiet about what he was doing, yet with all his efforts to remain anonymous, he still became one of the most famous people of all time.

Consider the day he fed over 5,000 people with only a few loaves! The locals would have been talking. In fact, in one of the accounts, they wanted to make him their king (John 6). At the time, this was easily the equivalent to going viral.

Jesus responds in the way we expect him to, with humility. He rejected the crowds, choosing to focus instead on discipleship, but the story isn't as simple as that.

Jesus has an interesting relationship with the crowds in the Gospel of Mark. He rejects them, runs away from them, and tries to avoid them. At the same time, he shows them love, has compassion for them, and does miracles that draw people to him in droves.

You can see this unique tension best by going to your favorite Bible website and searching for the word "crowd" in the NIV. Then narrow your search to the Gospel of Mark. What you will find is that in every occurrence of "crowd" in Mark, chapters 1-5, the crowds are set up in opposition to Jesus. They were in the way and were generally a nuisance. Often, Jesus tries to get away from the crowds. It's as if the crowds are a character in the story causing nothing but trouble. Then this troublemaker character changes, in one verse.

> When Jesus landed and saw a large crowd, he had compassion on them, because they were like sheep without a shepherd. So, he began teaching them many things. (Mark 6:34, NIV)

He had compassion on them, so he began teaching them.

Compassion leads to changed behavior.

A few hours later, he feeds them—once again making him popular and he has to escape to get away (Mark 5:4). The fame annoys him, causes trouble, but he loves them anyways, and because he loves them, they gather more, and then he has to escape again!

This is Jesus's relationship with popularity.

Christians are meant to be more and more like Jesus every day, but this love-hate relationship with crowds is hard to model. It's a struggle, especially for the progressive planter, who is called to "reach" people, but hates proselytizing. You want your church to grow, but you don't want to become a mega-church. You want authentic, close-knit communities, but you know better than to let the church exist only for yourselves. You know we need to help new people become a part of our church, but you hate the word "evangelism." If you want to be like Jesus, you should be doing things that get people's attention, but if you're going to be like Jesus, you can't do those things to get attention. It's complicated and nuanced.

If you've set out to launch a church, you will need to wrestle with this tension.

There's no better way to confront this than in exploring catalytic events. Jesus feeding the 5,000 is the perfect example of a catalytic event.

It's the only miracle that can be found in all four Gospels. Theologically, this is because setting a table is essential to the ministry of the church, but pragmatically, you could just as easily argue that it was such a newsworthy event that none of the Gospels could dream of leaving it out. The other miracles only include a few people, but if Jesus really came close to feeding over 5,000, everyone would know at least someone who had been there. You can't keep that kind of story under wraps. Because of this, let's take this passage and use it as a backdrop for understanding this idea of catalytic events.

I first heard of this term, "catalytic events," from Brad Aycock, Director of Fresh Starts and New Beginnings in the West Ohio Conference of the UMC, when I took his Greenhouse training for new church starts. The idea is simple: before launching, hold a newsworthy event that helps you introduce yourself to your community and meet new people.A catalytic event:

- is a one-time event that,
- connects with a large number of people,
- helps cast vision for the church,
- helps build your team, and
- is a story that people talk about.

Let's look at each of these in detail.

Is a One-Time Event

Obviously, there is nothing wrong with launching a ministry that is going to have a long-term impact. In fact, that is exactly what you should do, once you've launched. You should invest in and develop a signature local mission that takes the best practices of asset-based community development and community organizing and do it in a way where you are able to maintain and invest into it over a long period of time. But that isn't the same as a catalytic event. A catalytic event needs to be so big that it would be impossible for your small church plant to do it more than once or twice a year.

Jesus fed 5,000 people, but he only did this once—maybe twice. He couldn't do it every day and that's what made it a catalyst. If you could do it every week, it's not big enough.

After our church merged, we planned to hold a grand re-opening. Leading up to it, we were dreaming of what kind of event we could host that would help us catch a vision for the church we wanted to be. In the end, we decided to plan a *Bless Our City* event where we stocked all 100 blessing boxes in our city.

Blessing Boxes are free little pantries, where anyone can leave what they want or take what they need. They are small, often the size of a news stand or large mailbox and are in all kinds of places: in front of schools, businesses, homes, community centers, and churches. We reached out to the local organization that provided leadership for these blessing boxes and learned that there were over 100 in our community, often visited as many as five times a day by those in need.

A month leading up to our big event, we gathered supplies and donations from our church and community members. Using our mission's budget, we purchased what we needed to supplement the donations to ensure we had enough to make it worth it. We divided the boxes into routes, provided the addresses, and recruited drivers. Then our big day came. We gathered in our church fellowship hall the day before our grand re-opening and proceeded to pack 100 reusable grocery bags with dozens of supplies from soap to noodles to macaroni and cheese to snacks. An hour later, we sorted the bags and sent them out with the drivers. Each team drove throughout our city, literally blessing every corner in a tangible way.

Were we able to fill every blessing box every day of the year after that? No. But this one event grabbed people's attention, and helped our church and the wider community see a vision for what the church could be. Many people went on to fill boxes near where they lived, and when the local news did a story on the event, it inspired other people to do the same. This is a catalytic event. It's a one-time event that grabs people's attention and creates a story that people can't stop talking about.

Connects with a Large Number of People

It's interesting that scripture tells us how many people Jesus feeds. The reason is obvious: it's what made it a great story! He didn't just feed a family; he fed a crowd.

This is a great lesson. Jesus only had a worship attendance of twelve disciples but fed 5,000. Never let the numbers of your launch team dictate the dream you have for your community. And follow Jesus's example, taking more time talking about the impact you have had on people outside the church than bragging about the number of people you have inside the church.

A catalytic event is an event that can be measured in numbers. It's one of the few times scriptures encourages you to "go big."

When we did the blessing box event, we repeated how we were going to fill all *100* blessing boxes, covering the *entire* city. Filling one box is nice, but it's not a catalytic event.

A couple church plants in our conference held a week of service leading up to their launch. Their catalytic event lasted for more than a day, and they celebrated the number of hours and volunteers and organizations they served in their community. In the end, they were able to volunteer at dozens of local charities! Organizing volunteers for *one* charity is nice, but it's not a catalytic event.

Another church planter gathered volunteers in her church to package food for people struggling overseas. They packed 10,000 packages of food. Packing food for one person is nice, but it's not a catalytic event. But 10,000 packages of food?! That's worth talking about.

To go big, you need to consider your context.

Dave Warner, a church planter in Newark, Ohio, told me about how they'd hold a massive Easter egg hunt in collaboration with their city as their catalytic event. "This is a huge event for us on the Saturday before Easter. We can draw 200-300 families for these things! We capture email addresses for registrations and then we can send further invitations to them." This worked because their church and play cafe was located on the center square and there was an obvious need and opportunity in their community. Dave went on to say, "Basically we've always piggy backed off whatever is already going on in the city. We've never been strong enough to pull it off on our own but rather take advantage of people already gathering." Their church also launched a play cafe as their signature local ministry, so having events that were geared towards kids was essential. "If you bring the kids, you bring the adults," Dave said.

Tyler Kleeberger planted a church in rural northwest Ohio. Before launching, they held barn parties. They would bring in great music and amazing food trucks and gather in an old barn. Hundreds of people, from all walks of life, came to their barn parties. It looked like so much fun that I called him up and asked what advice he had for us doing something similar at our church. After a short phone conversation, I realized that this might not work in our context. Our church was in a major city with dozens of amazing restaurants and music venues. He explained that part of what made the barn parties work is there weren't a lot of great fine dining options or music venues in their rural county. Their church was able to scratch an itch and that's why people, many who didn't go to their church, came out to them.

One sure way to know you're meeting a need in the community is to see how many non-church people show up to your events. Outreach events that include mostly church people aren't outreach events.

Another church plant held a festival for one of their catalytic events. It was geared towards kids, with bounce houses and face painting and more. Turns out they did not have very many people, other than those in their church, show up. There's nothing more demoralizing to a launch team than an event that isn't well attended.

There are a couple of possible reasons why it didn't attract more people. While there were a lot of families in the area, very few lived directly next to the church. Their immediate neighbors were mostly empty nesters. Another reason had to do with the competing festivals. Their metropolitan area has amazing festivals every weekend in the summer, and these are done in ways small churches can't compete. This is a good lesson in planning a catalytic event. In order for it to be big, it can't compete with something that is already done well in your area.

Jon Morgan, from Hope Collective Church, didn't do a big event when they launched their church, for this very reason. He explained it like this: "There are enough events going on in the community that we don't need to create anything new. We show up to community events, being supportive however we can, and use those opportunities to interact with the community."

Jon is phenomenal at meeting new people and inviting them to church. His church is compassionate and invested in their community and so this model worked for them. For someone like me, who is more awkward or introverted, showing up to already-established events isn't as effective. In other words, you need to not only know your context, but your launch team's giftedness.

A festival, in a neighborhood that doesn't have one, might be a great fit, but one in an area where there's a festival every other weekend, it would be better to show up to what's already happening and try and come up with something different or unique to grab people's attention.

Helps Cast Vision for the Church

When Jesus fed the 5,000, he was doing more than meeting people's every day hunger. He was casting a vision for the kind of community he hoped to build: a community of people sharing what they have, making sure everyone has enough. It's no coincidence that this is exactly what the church became (Acts 2:44-45). It's as if Jesus's catalytic event helped shape their future reality.

One-time events are not the finish line, they're the starting place. They aren't the end goal; they are the spark that can move a community towards something bigger. They help people see what is possible. They help a church—and the wider community—move towards something better.

Jon, from Hope Collective, told me about another catalytic event he did at his previous church:

> At Fort McKinley, our most meaningful event was Kickball With the Cops. In our predominantly African American neighborhood, it was important for us to help the law enforcement and community build relationships. The cops and community were on teams together. It was a great representation of who we were as a church. It helped us build a lot of trust between the church and community as well.

This kind of event casts a vision for what the church could be! Just like feeding 5,000 shows us the kind of community Jesus was building or filling 100 blessing boxes reminds us that we're here to be a blessing to our city. The same is true for the week of service, showing the world that you want to serve the city. A big festival or block party can do that too, if you're trying to let people know you're a church that likes to have fun. A barn party can show people that meaningful relationships are possible even when miles of rural farmland keep people isolated. Catalytic events can help both your church, and the wider community catch a vision for what's possible.

Instead of trying to come up with a creative idea, start with your mission. What are you trying to accomplish and what good do you want to see in the world? For Jesus, we're given a picture in Revelation of a great feast (Revelation 19:11-13) as if this is the end goal Jesus had in mind. Feeding 5,000 is a one-time monumental event that gives us a glimpse of this vision.

What kind of church are you trying to plant?

How you reach people, is how you keep them, so what is your end goal? Be sure your big event points people in that direction.

If you want to have a fun church, throw a party. If you want to be a neighborhood church, find out what your neighborhood needs and do something big—or show up in force with what's happening already. If you want to see people across the political spectrum learn to love each other, hold a community conversation with significant leaders from both sides of the aisle engaging in healthy conversation. If you want to be a church for those in recovery, look up the 50 Alcoholic Anonymous groups in your area and provide each group with fancy coffee and donuts for their meeting one week.

A few other ideas to consider:

- **Gas giveaway:** Set up at a gas station and purchase gas for people who show up. Just be sure not to share this ahead of time to avoid potential traffic problems.
- **Free laundry:** Provide change, detergent, and folding laundry for people coming into the laundromats that morning
- **Help the elderly with work around their homes:** This may include washing outside windows and cleaning flower beds. You can work with a local senior citizen organization or something similar.

The ideas are endless.

Whatever you do, you're looking for something the wider community, outside your church, cares about. The 5,000 Jesus fed didn't all believe the same thing about God, but they all agreed free food was a good thing. Catalytic events aren't for the disciples, they are for the crowds, and should be inclusive of everyone, no matter what they believe. In other words, there is no need for an altar call or prayer vigil. You don't need to host a Christian artist or a praise and worship concert. Instead of doing something religious, find where your church's mission intersects with the hopes and dreams of those you hope to meet, and create something that the wider community is excited about. This will go a long way in helping your launch team and the wider community catch a vision of bringing God's kingdom to earth.

Helps Build Your Team

A new church has to take a group of strangers and make them into a family. There's no better way to build relationships than people working towards a common goal and serving together. One of the main points of the catalytic event is to get your launch team engaged in your church and comfortable serving together. For many church plants, a big event before the launch might be one of the first times they've volunteered together.

There are innumerable benefits to making sure your catalytic event gives your launch team places to serve.

First, this gives you something to ask people to do. As you meet with people during the launch season, but aren't offering worship services yet, it's great to have something to invite people to, and many people outside the church will show up to volunteer for a meaningful event before they show up to attend a worship service.

Second, relationships are forged. People will meet and make new friends in ways they never would have if you hadn't hosted this event. If your event is accomplished by a small group of pastors and staff, it can't be considered a success. A catalytic event is most successful when it gives people a chance to get involved and meet each other.

Third, this is the training ground for the church. Look at the story of feeding 5,000—Jesus didn't just pass out the loaves and fishes to everyone *himself*. He had his disciples do it. Not only were 5,000 people fed, but his disciples had their first lesson in food distribution and community organizing. When a food shortage happened amongst the most vulnerable in the early church (Acts 6), the disciples had the experience to empower others, just like Jesus had empowered them.

Catalytic events—or any part of this process—are a chance to help people learn how to be the church.

A Story People Talk About

Even though Jesus had a love-hate relationship with popularity, in the end, his stories were written down and passed along and have in turn, changed the world. Stories can do that. They give us a chance to imagine things differently.

It's not about doing good things in order to get a story written about you. In fact, Jesus is clear in the sermon on the mount (Matthew 6) that if you do good in the world in order to be seen by others, then you're no better than the corrupt religious leaders he condemned.

You shouldn't do good things to be seen, and if the only good your church does is what is covered in the news or on social media, you've missed the point. Having said that, it's fine and appropriate to allow and encourage people to tell the positive stories of what God is doing in your midst. Our world needs to know that good things are possible—that good things are already happening. Our world needs to know there are people of faith—like you—that love them just the way they are. The world needs these stories to combat all the other stories people have encountered in church.

There are a number of ways to share the story. At the very least, it's important to always have someone snapping photos and videos. Nowadays, it's easy to use photo programs to create simple videos to share in worship. It's recommended to do a catalytic event before your launch, so that a video can be shown at the service, celebrating what God has done. Stories like this keep the church moving forward and excited to be a part of this new community. Whether with videos or photos, it's the job of the pastor and other leaders to share stories with their congregation in every way possible: social media, sermons, worship, newsletters, etc.

The afternoon after our blessing box event, I got a text from one of our staff:

> We just saw a person walk up to the blessing box. They were so happy to see it full. They threw their hands up into the air with joy, kissed the box, and lifted their hands in a thankful posture to the sky. Then they

> ran over and hugged the tree right next to the blessing box and turned to our van and gave a big thumbs up with the biggest grin ever. It was awesome! I wish everyone who had been there this morning could have seen that!

This is a story worth telling. We shared this story in worship that Sunday and in our staff meeting. Stories like this are the *why* behind events like this.

Another time, I was working in our church's courtyard, not far from our blessing box. Someone came up to the box and me and a volunteer went over to chat with them. It turns out she was homeless, living not far from our church, and shared her appreciation for the box. I asked her if there was anything she wanted to see more of and she had some great suggestions. Then I asked her if having the blessing box here was useful, and she said, "It's probably the reason I'm still alive."

By themselves, little blessings boxes might not grab the attention of people disconnected from the church, but once they hear stories like this, it's hard not to care.

God will give you these experiences to share with others. Its why Revelation says that we will overcome evil in this world through the work of Jesus on the cross and our personal stories of transformation (Revelation 12:11).

Imagine how the families who went out of their way to donate, volunteer, or deliver supplies will feel when they hear a story like this!

One of the great things about catalytic events is that often the local news wants to cover it. If you've never gotten the news to cover your ministry, here are a few tips and tricks to get you started.

Working with Local News

What follows is great advice for getting your catalytic event covered by your local news. Please don't abuse this—motivation matters. The goal isn't to make the church or your pastor look good. The goal is to inspire the wider community to catch a vision of what God can do when we all come together.

You can do this in a few ways.

First, always talk about the good already happening in your community. Whatever good you do in the world, others have likely been doing similar work for years. Mention and celebrate those who have laid the groundwork for your event. If you do an event filling blessing boxes, talk about the people and organization who have been doing it for years. If you partner with a food bank to do a citywide collection, make the story about the food bank more than your church. If you're doing an Easter egg hunt in the city square, talk about how great your community is and all those who hold similar events.

Second, it's ok to include information about your church. Don't hide that you're a church or pretend like people don't want to know. The goal here is to let people know that your church is committed to doing good in the world, and rest assured that there are people in your community looking for a church like that. Don't hide who you are. Be honest, humble, but outgoing with this information.

Third, find the right angle. No matter how exciting your event is, it's likely not newsworthy. Your event, by itself, isn't the story. At best, it's the launching point for the story. This is especially true for large cities. Unless you have significant contacts in the local news and can pull some favors, most events a church plant pulls off won't be newsworthy in and of itself.

You need to be more creative than that.

For example, when our church launched, and we got a story in the local paper, the actual story was about church attendance decline in the nation, the struggle of denominations, and how our denomination was investing in church planting. That was the story, but the photo was me and my wife Allyssa standing in front of the Grandview Theater with a caption talking about our upcoming launch. In the end, we had lots of visitors check out our church because of that story.

The same is true when we got the blessing box event covered. Coming out of COVID, food insecurity had increased, and blessing boxes was one way our church could address that issue.

The story they told was about food insecurity and how people can donate to blessing boxes. The fact that our church was filling all 100 boxes at our event was a footnote to the actual story.

When inviting the press, take time to think about your event in this way. Include in your pitch the reason why your event responds to current or national issues.

Along with being a pastor, I serve as the president of the Ohio Writers' Association. We recently did an anthology of short stories called *Should This Book Be Banned?* The idea was to collect stories about and from people and ideas that are often overlooked or marginalized. When I reached out to the local news to cover the story, I explained that this anthology was in response to the banning of books happening nationwide. By connecting this anthology to the national news, we had two local news sources run a story.

Most recently, our church has gotten involved in violence reduction and as such, I've interacted with the local news often. While the news might ask about our event or violence reduction campaign, they always turn the conversation and ask us to address a *recent* homicide. This is how the news works; they want to talk about an event *in light of* what is already happening. So, when inviting the local news to an event, help your local news connect the dots between your event and the issues they want to cover.

Fourth, pitch your story in a clear, concise way. The easiest way to do this is to write a press release, even if you only use it informally. Include a headline, date, time, location, brief overview, quote, and contact information. Whether you write it up as a formal press release with your church's letterhead or just a note that you can copy and paste into emails, the important thing is that you put yourself out there. Take time to learn the emails and phone numbers of media personalities in your area. As stories come up in your church, send them your ideas. You won't' get a response to every story—like every other part of church planting, you have to keep going until something takes root.

If you're starting out without any contacts, it's as easy as looking up the local news stations and magazines online. If you scroll to the bottom of most of their pages or go to their "contact us" page, there will be a place to submit a story suggestion. You can't do this for every event—and it would be unwise to be too aggressive—but if you're launching a new church, holding a big event to introduce yourself to the community, or having some other event in the future or cause that is gaining national attention, it's worth trying. Remember, the great commandment for church planters is this: *You have not, because you ask not.* Put yourself out there.

Reflection

A newsworthy event is a great way to introduce your church to a community and can go a long way to connecting with new people. It can be a lot of work, but if done well, it can help you launch. Take a few minutes to reflect and dream about your catalytic event.

1. What is the biggest barrier for doing a catalytic event? What ideas do you have for overcoming these obstacles?
2. Where does your mission intersect with things your community cares about? Consider using this Venn diagram:

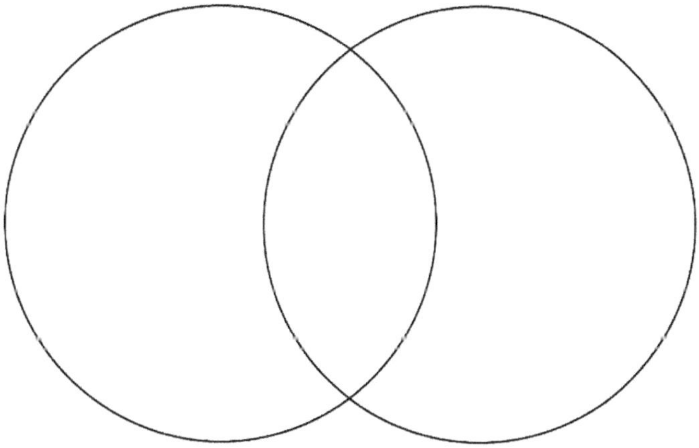

   a. In the first circle, write out your church plant's mission. What is the *why* behind your church? Jesus feeding 5,000 pointed people to the Eucharist, the heavenly banquet, and an equitable community where all have enough to eat. What event could help people in your community see the vision for your church?

b. In the second circle, write out some of the values you know your community cares about. If you haven't already, use demographic reports like MissionInsite or others to learn your communities' values.

c. In the overlapping section, consider what parts of your mission intersect with things your community cares about.

d. What event could exist in this intersection that both your church and the wider community would be excited about?

e. Write down as many ideas as you can.

f. Of these ideas, which ones:

    i. Are overdone…

    ii. Too complicated/difficult to pull off…

    iii. Not big enough…

    iv. Give the wrong impressions…

3. When you have an idea, consider how it meets these goals:

    a. What's the number you could celebrate? Is it how many people you serve or the number of volunteers; or is it the number of boxes you fill, give away, or package? Or something else?

    b. How does this event paint a picture of what your church wants to be about?

    c. Will your launch team be excited about this and give time and energy to making it happen?

    d. What kind of story will this event turn into? Do you think it's newsworthy?

Church Planter's Toolkit

Go to churchplantershandbook.org to access the following resources related to this chapter:

- **Catalytic Event Worksheet:** Use this worksheet to develop a plan for your catalytic event.
- **Event Marketing Checklist:** This checklist, broken into the weeks leading up to an event, provides dozens of ideas on how to market not only your catalytic event, but your Launch Sunday and any other future events.
- **Post-Event Reflection Worksheet:** Use this guide to evaluate the effectiveness of your event across 9 different categories.

Chapter 13

Launch Day & Every Day After

When the day of Pentecost came, they were all together in one place.
—Acts 2:1

After Jesus ascended into heaven, the disciples joined in with their Jewish brothers and sisters for the festival of Pentecost, a holiday where the Hebrew people celebrated the fall harvest. This festival occurred on the 50th day, or seven weeks after Passover, thus becoming known as Pentecost, from the Greek *pentēkostē* ("50th").

In an agricultural world, a successful harvest meant another year of life. The harvest represented days and days of hard labor, stress, and pain. Taking time to stop and celebrate a successful harvest was only logical.

It's at this celebration of the harvest that God's Spirit falls on the disciples, and it couldn't happen at a more appropriate time. All their labors and training and work would finally produce its own harvest. The disciples would finally see the fruit of their labors. As Paul would later articulate, the disciples could only plant and water the seeds; they had no ability to make something grow. The same would be true for the Church. It was the Spirit of God falling on the people that gave them the harvest they were longing for.

God's Spirit moves and blows like the wind, often unexpected and free from boundaries (John 3:8). The wind doesn't ask permission or seek approval. It is the same for the Spirit. Yet, in all the ways God could have given birth to the Church, God did it when everyone was together in one place.

That's often the case. God loves to show up in profound ways when people are in the room together.

Launch Day gives church planters their own Pentecost experiences. This was true for both Central City and Open Church.

Launch Day at Central City Church

On Sunday morning, I got up early, making final edits to my sermon. My wife and I were pastoring together, having just had Finn not long before. I kissed Allyssa and Finn goodbye and went to the theater. They would meet me there later.

We launched out of a small historic theater located right in the middle of our community. We had to set everything up, but thankfully we had three preview services which were great rehearsals for our Launch Day and a way to measure how well we connected with the neighborhood. Preview services, or similar events, are essential to a successful launch.

We stacked the tables and chairs behind the bar and set up our children's space on one side and our nursery on the other. For years, people joked that our children's space happened in a bar!

Our band set up the drums and a small stage for me to preach from. We pulled in our hospitality cart, and volunteers started to make coffee.

That morning, we gathered our volunteers before the service to pray. At least twenty people from our launch tram were standing in a circle, holding hands, praying for this day.

It was beautiful.

By the second song, the theater was full of people, and so were our hearts. Our church was born.

A few things to keep in mind if your church centers around a weekly worship service:

- **You're going to be exhausted.** Go into the day as prepared as you can, so you can sit back and relax. This model of church planting builds up over time and by the time your big day comes, you'll be tired. Take time off after the service.

- **Perfection isn't the goal; excellence is.** Do your best and train your team to do the same. Take as much time as you need in the launch season to properly prepare for this service. Visit like-minded or similar churches and take pages of notes from what you observe. Turn these notes into launch team trainings, so everyone is on the same page when your big day comes.
- **Iteration is your greatest tool.** Constantly seek evaluation and feedback, making changes as quickly as you can. Traditions are started quickly in communities. It only takes a few weeks of doing something for people to think "That's how we've always done it." Experiment and make changes where you see the need as quickly as possible.

Launch Day at Open Church

Seven years later, Allyssa found herself with a similar morning. She got up early, working on the final touches of her sermon, but instead of going to her Launch Day worship service, she went to a church down the street. A friend she had been mentoring was getting baptized that morning and the pastor had invited Allyssa to participate in the service. She was able to be there for the baptism on the same Sunday her church launched because her church wasn't launching a church centered around a Sunday service. She launched a network of microchurches. Her Launch Day was a *commissioning service* for the seven microchurch leaders who were launching their own fresh expressions that met throughout the week. This commissioning service would happen later in the afternoon.

Open Church's commissioning service gathered in an old church that has been intricately woven into our story, now owned and operated by a local charter school. It wasn't far from my house, so Finn and I hopped on our tandem bike and rode over, the fall wind pushing against us so much that the short blocks felt like miles. We locked the bike up just outside the church building and went inside.

What followed started as a standard service, with worship and singing, except it culminated when the seven microchurch leaders came forward and shared their hopes and dreams. From there, they were sent with a blessing to be the hands and feet of Jesus and another church was born.

A few things to keep in mind when launching a unique expression of church:

- **Church is More Than a Worship Service**: Open Church's story shows a different, but equally valid, launch model. Church planting isn't just about filling a room on Sundays—it's about creating sustainable expressions of faith that multiply and serve in diverse ways. A church isn't defined by a single day but by the movement it sustains. The real work begins after launch.
- **Make Room for Others to Lead:** The job of clergy is "to equip the saints for the work of ministry" (Ephesians 4:11). Church planting isn't about a pastor's platform; it's about equipping and releasing leaders to create new expressions of faith.
- **People will be confused.** People are used to what they are used to. It takes a lot longer to show people what's possible if you're significantly deviating from what is considered the "standard" for that population. This is true for any church pushing against denominational, cultural, or racial status quos and expectations. Lean into discipleship, taking time with people over a long period to properly prepare them for what this will look like.
- **Funding Needs to Match the Model.** A home-based church led by a layperson is sustainable if they are willing to lead without compensation. A house church lead by a full-time clergy, with benefits, is not sustainable. The cost and income of a church model must match, eventually. When exploring new expressions of church, do the hard work of figuring out your funding strategy. A network of lay-driven ministries lead by a full-time clergy can be sustainable, if intentional work is done to create generous givers in those communities and there are sufficient funds at the start.

Chapter 13

A Second Look at Pentecost

Those who accepted his message were baptized, and about three thousand were added to their number that day.—Acts 2:41

3,000 were added to their number! At first glance, you could assume this is evidence of the first mega-church! Isn't this what God wants to do when the Spirit is unleashed? Not quite. Here's what was really going on.

Jews from all over the Roman Empire (v. 9-10) were coming to Jerusalem for the Festival of Pentecost. Peter preached and 3,000 were saved, but that doesn't mean they built a building so they could gather all 30,00 together. Instead, they were quickly dispersed, many returning to their hometowns with the good news of Jesus.

To understand just how significant this event was, you need to go all the way back to the opening chapters of Genesis.

The Tower of Babel is a prehistoric story of Israel and one that needs to be considered again. The people all spoke the same language and shared the same culture and grew powerful. They had built a massive mega-church—or towner—with the hope to reach God. They came together, in large numbers, and God wasn't happy in the end. God tried to correct their course by introducing languages to confuse them and push them to embrace different cultures, scattering them.

Diversity is a gift from God. It's the way God envisioned this world.

Pentecost is the great reversal of the Tower of Babel. Instead of people building a tower to reach God, God descended on the people. Instead of everyone learning to be the same, speaking the same and being forced to adapt to the same culture, God spoke to them in their native languages and cultures. Instead of building a tower to hold all 3,000 people, they went back to their hometowns, taking the gospel with them.

This story teaches that the faster a church grows, the better it must be at sending people. It's a lesson Open Church has taken seriously and should challenge all of us to do the same.

A church's success isn't in attendance but in its ability to be the church in the neighborhoods and streets God has called it to, sending people out to be God's hands and feet there. It's in the transformation that happens in individuals' lives, that they might bring about transformation in the world. It's only when our new churches model the prophetic tradition of Pentecost, gathering people to send them out, that we begin to understand the true purpose of the church.

If sending people is at the heart of the church's mission, then your launch service should reflect that from the very beginning. A well-planned launch service isn't just about gathering a crowd—it's about setting the tone for a church that intends to change the world for the better. That's why every element of your launch service should reinforce the vision of a church that exists for the transformation of both its people and its community. So, how do you design a launch service with this mission in mind? Here are five key goals to guide you.

5 Goals for a Launch Service

1. **Clearly communicate your vision & mission:** The only way to invite people into something new is to share your vision for what that *new* might look like. As you gather for your Launch Day, share those vision stories you've written, let people know how your church came about, and use these to paint a picture of where you're headed.

> Growing Generous Givers
>
> As you plan your Launch Day, or any other gathering, how will you talk about giving? And for those interested in giving, how can they give? Is there a place they can leave a check or cash? Is there a link or QR code to donate online? Go into your gatherings with a clear plan so those who want to donate, can.

2. **Provide an authentic experience that represents who you want to be:** If you're launching a weekly worship service, then make sure your Launch Day reflects what your weekly service is aspiring to be. If you're a missional community, your Launch Day better be

acts of mission and service. Are you a network of microchurches or fresh expressions? Consider a commissioning service like Allyssa did. Whatever you do, ensure your worship and teaching reflects the kind of church you hope to be and it's done with the level of quality people could expect if they started attending weeks after the launch.

The best way to ensure this is to have either preview services or a couple of rehearsals before Launch Day, to ensure your launch team has had time to become comfortable with the rhythms of your new worship service. It's only after people experience something, reflect on it, and are invited to evaluate it that they will see the ways it can be improved. Preview services or rehearsals with clear evaluation processes are essential for this process.

3. **Practice radical hospitality:** To do hospitality well in a new church, focus on creating a warm, inclusive environment where every person feels seen and valued. This begins with intentionality—greet newcomers personally, offer clear signage and accessible spaces, and ensure follow-up to make them feel remembered. Train your hospitality team to be attentive without being overwhelming, helping visitors feel comfortable and at ease. Provide simple, thoughtful touches like refreshments, clean and inviting spaces, and opportunities for meaningful connection. Most importantly, foster a culture where hospitality extends beyond the Sunday service, ensuring that care, community, and welcome are ongoing experiences for all.

4. **Celebrate:** This is a great time to throw a party, have something fun, or offer a special treat. On Central City's Launch Day, we ordered locally-made, organic frozen fruit bars. We didn't know it, but next to the theater was a coffee house. Someone watched people walk by with these frozen treats and asked where they got them from. They told them they were being passed out by the church that met in the theater. "There's a church that is meeting in a theater! Passing out popsicles?! Doesn't that theater have a bar in it?" Yes, it does. Charlie started attending the next week, intrigued by this new church, all because someone walked by with a fancy popsicle. Years later, she served on our board, eventually becoming the board chair. Her gifts in leadership carried our church through a season of conflict and

then the merger, becoming the first board chair at Cityview Church. But what if we hadn't had those popsicles?

Don't underestimate the power of having fun.

5. **Provide clear and concise steps for those who want to get involved:** Will you be offering an event to learn more? Do they need to fill out an online form or connect card? Do you have gifts for visitors? Are there opportunities to serve or get involved?

When Peter preached his life-changing message in Acts chapter 2, the next paragraph tells us what happened in the community of those who stayed in Jerusalem. Whether you've read this passage before, or not, read it with fresh eyes, looking for examples of what "next steps" you might offer those who attend your Launch Day.

> 42 They devoted themselves to the apostles' teaching and to fellowship,
> to the breaking of bread and to prayer. 43 Everyone was filled with awe
> at the many wonders and signs performed by the apostles. 44 All the
> believers were together and had everything in common. 45 They sold
> property and possessions to give to anyone who had need. 46 Every day
> they continued to meet together in the temple courts. They broke bread
> in their homes and ate together with glad and sincere hearts, 47 praising
> God and enjoying the favor of all the people. And the Lord added to
> their number daily those who were being saved. (Acts 2:42-47)

The birth of the church wasn't the end of the story, it was the beginning. It launched this new community into a life together, committed to loving each other and their neighbors. Imagine if Pentecost was a modern church on their Launch Day, with music and preaching and announcements—yes, *announcements*! It's easy to imagine that they'd have announcements like these:

- "Small groups and classes now enrolling! Here is a list of small groups and classes we have, to help you grow in your faith." (verses 42 and 44)
- "We love caring for our community. If you need prayer or some kind of tangible resource during a difficult time, please let us

know. We have a care ministry budget that is used to help people in our community." (v. 43)

- "If you'd like to give towards this ministry, you can leave a check or cash in the Dropbox, go to our website and click on 'give,' or scan the QR code on your handout. It's through generous gifts like yours that enable us to be the church in our city." (v. 45)
- "Sign up to join us for our next volunteer opportunity serving our city! We will be sorting, packing and distributing food to the free little pantries in our neighborhood. You can sign up to volunteer on the connect card." (v. 45)
- "Join us next week as we begin our new sermon series. We're going to talk about what it will look like for us to become the church." (v. 46)
- "We're having a Post-Launch Party at our pastor's house, and we'd love to have you come join us for a chance to meet people and share a meal together." (v. 46)
- "If you'd like to learn more about following Jesus or being baptized, please sign the connect card. We'd love to help you take the next step of faith today." (v. 47)

These are just examples of what is possible. In the end, use your Launch Day to do more than just start weekly services. It's an invitation into a new community with a clear mission.

Now What?

It's a question that often plagues someone after they've worked on a project all the way to completion. They're tired and exhausted, and they sit on the steps of the building after everyone else has gone, and they wonder, "Now what?"

Where do you go from here?

The first step is to breathe and rest. Everything up to this point will have a toll on you and your launch team. Take time to get away and take time off. In fact, schedule your vacation after the launch months before, so you have something to look forward to.

What happens if the launch isn't "successful"? Well, that just depends on what you mean by *successful*. If you've gathered a few new people who seem energetic about your vision and mission, work with that. If you've done your best and been faithful to God's call on your life, then it's been *successful*. If you have gathered fewer people than you *hoped*, that has more to do with expectations than success. If you've gathered fewer people than you *need* to be sustainable, you might have more work to do. You might not be able to start practicing church as-is, but you can work with the people you have and keep moving forward. Remember, church planting is *people building*. Keep meeting people and inviting them to join you. Keep building a group of people who are willing to chase God's dreams together. Keep working the steps, sharing the vision, adjusting your plans, and trying out your ideas and God will take care of the rest.

Let's say the launch is "successful," and you've gathered as many as you hoped—maybe more!—and you need to start figuring out how to build all the systems that make a church a church. You're starting to think about discipleship, small groups, expanding your children's ministry, a signature local mission, generosity and stewardship, community organizing and collaborative partnership, or engaging in local justice movements—and everything in between. All of that and more will need to be done. Get started and know that God's blessing is with you!

Wherever you find yourself, be encouraged. Breathe in and breathe out. It's going to be ok.

Celebrate. Give thanks to God and those who came alongside you to make it reality.

If God brought you this far, rest assured God won't leave you now.

No, God's just getting started.

My Son's Birthday

On September 17, 2017, our new church launched weekly services. It's a date I'll always remember, because it happened to be Finn's first birthday. Initially, we worried that as a pastor's kid, sharing a birthday with our church, might cause some unresolved trauma in Finn's life.

Thankfully, that hasn't been the case—so far. In the end, our church has gone on to launch other ministries, my wife left to launch two other churches, and our church plant has merged with an established church, which means we don't even celebrate that launch date in any significant way.

September 17 is now dedicated only to our son. It's *his* birthday—but I still remember that first Sunday.

Our communication intern back then was also a great photographer, and I love going back and looking at the photos from that event. There's one that stands out more than the others

A few friends had brought gifts to my son, knowing it was his birthday. In typical one-year-old fashion, he was more interested in the tinsel used to fill the gift bag than the actual gift inside. There's this beautiful photo of Finn playing with this tinsel. It's just outside the Grandview Theater, moments after the service concluded, and it captures well the feeling people had as they were leaving. Finn was so happy. His cheeks were plump and his eyes bright, and he was jumping up and down as he played with this silver tinsel reflecting in the bright sun.

It's one of my favorite pictures of Finn.

It reminds me of the joy that came not only from watching him grow up but watching our church grow up. Finn, like our church, has grown a lot in the last seven years, and both have come with surprises. It turns out planting a church, like raising a child, has beautiful joy-filled moments, but overwhelmingly painful ones as well. In both, I have felt inadequate, underprepared, and quite frankly scared out of my mind. Still, through it all, God has remained faithful.

And the same will be true for you.

You can rest assured; God is with you.

Church Planter's Toolkit

Go to churchplantershandbook.org to access the following resources related to this chapter:

- **Launch Day Checklist:** Use this checklist to ensure you're ready for your big day!
- **Event Marketing Checklist:** This checklist, broken into the weeks leading up to an event, provides dozens of ideas on how to market your Launch Sunday and any other future events.
- **Post-Event Reflection Worksheet:** Use this guide to evaluate the effectiveness of your Launch Sunday across 9 different categories.

To access the Church Planter's Toolkit at
churchplantershandbook.org,enter this passcode:
PLANT!TOOLS

Notes

Chapter 1. Reasons to Plant a Church (and Reasons Not To)

1. Jessica Estrada, "'Trauma Drive' explains why a loss of motivation may just be sign of healing," Well+Good, https://www.wellandgood.com/health/trauma-drive (2022 May 7).

2. Anna Steinhage, Dan Cable, and Duncan Wardley, "The Pros and Cons of Competition Among Employees," *Harvard Business Review,* https://hbr.org/2017/03/the-pros-and-cons-of-competition-among-employees (2017 March 20).

Chapter 3. Ministry Action Plan

1. David Kinnaman and Aly Hawkins, *You Lost Me: Why Young Christians Are Leaving Church . . . and Rethinking Faith* (Baker, 2016).

Chapter 5. Prayer

1. Based on the book *The Four Pages of a Sermon* by Paul Scott Wilson (Abingdon, 2010).

Chapter 6. Meeting New People

1. "Grassroots Organizing," The United Methodist Church: Church and Society, https://www.umcjustice.org/what-you-can-do/grassroots-organizing (accessed 2025 April 11).

2. Jim Collins, *Good to Great and the Social Sectors: Why Business Thinking Is Not the Answer* (Harper Business, 2006).

3. Warren Bird, *Funding: What Does It Cost to Launch a New Church or Campus?* (n.d.).

Chapter 8. Recruiting Leaders

1. "More than 11 million people volunteered on an average day in 2022," The Economics Daily: US Bureau of Labor Statistics, https://www.bls.gov/opub/ted/2024/more-than-11-million-people-volunteered-on-an-average-day-in-2022.htm (2024 April 24).

2. "Volunteer: Participate in the Tradition of Volunteering," Network for Good, https://www.networkforgood.org/volunteer/volunteertradition.aspx (accessed 2025 April 4).

3. Barna Group, *Church Startups and Money: The Myths and Realities of Church Planters and Finances* (Barna Group, 2016).

Chapter 10. Marketing & Branding

1. Neil Postman, *Technopoly: the Surrender of Culture to Technology* (Vintage, 1993), 3–5.

2. "The Search for a New Congregation," Pew Research Center, https://www.pewresearch.org/religion/2016/08/23/1-the-search-for-a-new-congregation/#be10d244ff20fef0092fc926fba7d6f1 (2016 August 23).

3. Tony Morgan, "Differences between Growing & Declining Churches: Ministry Reach," The Unstuck Group, https://theunstuckgroup.com/differences-growing-declining-churches-ministry-reach/ (2018 May 1).

4. "The medium is the message" is a phrase coined by the Canadian communication theorist Marshall McLuhan and the name of the first chapter in his *Understanding Media: The Extensions of Man*, published in 1964.

5. ARC Launch Training, Association of Related Churches, https://www.arcchurches.com/equip/arc-launch-training/ (2024 December 5).

Chapter 11. Location, Location, Location

1. Timothy Keller, *Why Plant Churches* (Redeemer Presbyterian Church, 2002), http://download.redeemer.com/pdf/learn/resources/Why_Plant_Churches-Keller.pdf (accessed 2014 June 4).

2. Keller, *Why Plant Churches.*

3. Lyle E. Schaller, *44 Questions for Church Planters* (Abingdon 1991).

4. Ed Stetzer, Micah Fries, and Daniel Im, "The State of Church Planting in the US," https://www.wesleyan.org/wp-content/uploads/Lifeway-2015-ChurchPlanting-Survey.pdf (Life Way Research and NewChurches.com, 2015).

www.ingramcontent.com/pod-product-compliance
Lightning Source LLC
LaVergne TN
LVHW022024030525
810278LV00010B/24